Ending the Troubles

REACTING TO THE PAST is an award-winning series of immersive role-playing games that actively engage students in their own learning. Students assume the roles of historical characters and practice critical thinking, primary source analysis, and argument, both written and spoken. Reacting games are flexible enough to be used across the curriculum, from first-year general education classes and discussion sections of lecture classes to capstone experiences, intersession courses, and honors programs.

Reacting to the Past was originally developed under the auspices of Barnard College and is sustained by the Reacting Consortium of colleges and universities. The Consortium hosts a regular series of conferences and events to support faculty and administrators.

NOTE TO INSTRUCTORS: Before beginning the game you must download the game materials, including an instructor's manual containing a detailed schedule of class sessions, role sheets for students, and handouts.

To download these essential resources, visit https://reactingconsortium.org/games, click on the page for this title, then click "Game Materials."

Ending the Troubles

RELIGION, NATIONALISM, AND THE SEARCH FOR PEACE AND DEMOCRACY IN NORTHERN IRELAND, 1997–1998

JOHN M. BURNEY AND
ANDREW J. AUGE

BARNARD

The University of North Carolina Press

Chapel Hill

© 2024 Reacting Consortium, Inc.
All rights reserved

Cover art: *IRA Patrol in West Belfast, 1988*.
Courtesy of Pacemaker Press International.

ISBN 9781469683362 (pbk.: alk. paper)
ISBN 9781469683379 (epub)
ISBN 9781469683386 (pdf)

Contents

List of Illustrations / vii

1. INTRODUCTION / 1

Brief Overview of the Game / 1

Prologue / 2

Basic Features of Reacting to the Past / 6

    Game Setup / 6

    Game Play / 6

    Game Requirements / 7

    Controversy / 7

    Counterfactuals / 8

2. HISTORICAL BACKGROUND / 9

Chronology / 9

Overview of the Troubles / 11

The English in Ireland / 16

    The Origins of the English in Ireland / 16

    The Protestant Ascendency / 18

    The Growth of Cultural Nationalisms in the Nineteenth and Twentieth Centuries / 20

    The Home Rule Crisis and Rebellion / 22

The Development of Two Irelands / 28

    Solidifying Two Separate National Communities: Southern and Northern Ireland after 1922 / 28

The Troubles, 1967–1998 / 31

    The 1960s Civil Rights Movement and the Beginning of the Troubles / 31

    Direct Rule from Great Britain / 35

    Changing Strategies: Ulsterization, Criminalization, and the Hunger Strikes / 37

    Anglo-Irish Connections and the Opening to Negotiations / 38

    The Current Moment, June 1997 / 42

    Issues to Be Debated in the Multiparty Talks / 42

3. THE GAME / 45

Major Issues for Debate / 45

The Basic Questions: Nationalism and Democracy / 45

Competing Ideas and Cultures / 46

Terminology and Political Options / 51

Key Terms Used in the Game / 51

The Range of Options for a Political Solution / 51

Rules and Procedures / 53

Chair / 54

Proposals and Debate / 54

Voting / 54

Press Conferences and Public Opinion / 55

Marches / 55

Visual and Written Imagery / 56

Violence / 56

Coalition Building / 56

Assignments / 56

Objectives and Victory Conditions / 56

Other Considerations and Advice / 57

Basic Outline of the Game / 58

Setup and Context Sessions / 58

Game Begins / 58

Referendum and Debriefing / 60

4. ROLES AND FACTIONS / 63

Chairs / 64

Government Representatives / 64

Unionists / 64

Nationalists / 65

Cross-Community Parties / 65

5. CORE TEXTS / 67

Section A. Defending Cultural Communities: Personal Motives for Sectarian and Political War / 67

1. "Bernadette Devlin on Loyalist Ambush at Burntollet," 1969 / 68

2. Motivation for Joining the IRA: Excerpts from Kevin Toolis's *Rebel Hearts* / 69

3. Motivation for Loyalist Violence: Excerpts from Peter Taylor's *Loyalists* / 70

4. Bobby Sands, "The Harvest Britain Has Sown" / 70

5. The Day-to-Day Sectarian Tension of the Troubles: Excerpts from Kevin Toolis's *Rebel Hearts* / 71

Section B. Competing Concepts of Nationalism: Unionism and Loyalism / 72

6. The Ulster Covenant, 1912 / 72

7. James Craig, Parliamentary Speech: "A Protestant Government for Protestant People," 21 November 1934 / 73

8. Letter from the Orange Order to the Catholic Residents of the Garvaghy Road, 4 June 1997 / 73

9. Progressive Unionist Party: Excerpts from "The Principles of Loyalism" / 74

Section C. Competing Concepts of Nationalism: Nationalism and Republicanism / 80

10. Irish Nationalism: Excerpts from the Writings of Patrick Pearse, 1913–1916 / 80

11. The Easter Rising Proclamation, 1916 / 82

12. Excerpt from the Constitution of Ireland, Adopted 1937 / 83

13. Eamon de Valera's Vision of the Irish Republic, 1943 / 84

14. Excerpt from *Northern Ireland: The Plain Truth*, 2nd ed., 1969 / 84

15. The IRA Green Book: Guerrilla Strategy, 1977 / 85

Section D. Documents on the Multiparty Talks / 87

16. Joint Declaration on Peace: The Downing Street Declaration, 1993 / 87

17. The Paramilitary Ceasefire Announcements, 1994 / 89

18. Consultation Paper: Ground Rules for Substantive All-Party Negotiations Issued by the British Government, 15 March 1996 / 90

19. The "Mitchell Principles," or "Principles of Democracy and Non-violence," 1996 / 92

20. Excerpts from the Charter of Fundamental Rights of the European Union, 2000 / 93

Section E. Unionist Political Documents of the 1990s / 94

21. Ian Paisley Speech to the Democratic Unionist Party's Annual Conference, 1994 / 94

22. David Ervine Speech to the Progressive Unionist Conference, 1997 / 99

23. David Trimble Speech at the Annual General Meeting of the Ulster Unionist Council, 1996 / 100

Section F. Nationalist Political Documents of the 1990s / 103

24. Excerpt from John Hume's Leader's Address to the Social Democratic and Labour Party 25th Annual Conference, 1995 / 103

25. Excerpts from John Hume's *A New Ireland* / 103

26. Gerry Adams Speech to the Sinn Féin Ard Fheis (Annual Party Conference), 1994 / 105

27. Gerry Adams Speech to Sinn Féin Ard Fheis (Annual Party Conference), 1997 / 111

Section G. Cross-Community Political Document of the 1990s / 114

28. Alliance Party of Northern Ireland, "Multiparty Talks: Principles and Realities of a Settlement," 13 October 1997 / 114

Images of the Troubles: Where to Find Films, Murals, and Photographs / 116

Acknowledgments / 117

Notes / 119

Selected Bibliography / 121

The British Isles / 12
Northern Ireland / 13
English and Scottish Plantations of Ireland, 1620 / 17
Distribution of religions in Belfast / 47

Maps

Abbreviations

APNI	Alliance Party of Northern Ireland
DUP	Democratic Unionist Party
GM	game manager or game master
IRA	Irish Republican Army
IRB	Irish Republican Brotherhood
LVF	Loyalist Volunteer Force
MP	member of Parliament
NIO	Northern Ireland Office
NIWC	Northern Ireland Women's Coalition
PUP	Progressive Unionist Party
RUC	Royal Ulster Constabulary
SDLP	Social Democratic and Labour Party
SF	Sinn Féin
UDA	Ulster Defense Association
UDP	Ulster Democratic Party
UDR	Ulster Defence Regiment
UFF	Ulster Freedom Fighters
UKUP	United Kingdom Unionist Party
UUP	Ulster Unionist Party
UVF	Ulster Volunteer Force

Ending the Troubles

1

Introduction

BRIEF OVERVIEW OF THE GAME

In June 1996, after thirty years of bloody conflict, the British government under Prime Minister John Major convened multiparty talks to try to "achieve a new beginning for relationships within Northern Ireland, among the people of the island of Ireland and between the people of these islands." Chaired by former US senator George Mitchell, the talks invited all Unionist and Nationalist parties who had committed to "peaceful and democratic means" to define the constitutional position of Northern Ireland and to find new arrangements on the key relationships— in Strand 1: within Northern Ireland; Strand 2: within the whole of the island of Ireland; and Strand 3: between the British and Irish governments. Underneath these issues were fundamental questions of national identity and democracy. Those talks bogged down in the discussions of procedural issues and conflict over the principle of decommissioning—that paramilitaries must give up all their weapons in a verifiable fashion. Since the Irish Republican Army had resumed a bombing campaign in 1996 after a brief ceasefire, the party that was seen as connected to the IRA, Sinn Féin, was barred from the talks. Frustration rose in all quarters as the talks failed to produce any substantive progress.

The election of Tony Blair as the British prime minister with a clear Labour Party majority in the British Parliament in May 1997 has provided the opportunity to reenergize the talks. Players will represent the major parties in Northern Ireland as they reconvene at the multiparty talks in 1997 to confront the issue of decommissioning and to try to make progress on discussion of the three strands. Much is at stake, for another failure could lead to a full resumption of the civil war.

This game is designed for you to experience the tensions caused by the conflict of two national communities during the Troubles, to learn the motivations of the competing groups that struggled over the choice between continued war or political compromise, and to understand the processes that could produce a peace settlement in 1997–98. By the end of the game, you should learn and be able to do the following:

1. Understand the religious, cultural, political, and economic issues that contributed to conflict in Northern Ireland from 1968 to 1998.
2. Explain the processes and articulate the areas of compromise that led to the Good Friday Peace Agreement.
3. Utilize the concepts of civic and cultural nationalism to examine political conflict in Northern Ireland and the modern world.
4. Articulate the major challenges and opportunities posed for democratic constitutional arrangements in attempting to guarantee equal treatment of different national communities.

Ending the Troubles is designed to teach academic and civic skills that include critical thinking, persuasive writing and speaking, debate, and coalition building in an active learning environment. It will take you back to the roles of the major players and political parties in the negotiations that took place in Northern Ireland in 1997 and 1998, where you will have in your hands the potential for peace or for continuing war.

Note that this text will use the British spelling of words such as "defence" when they appear in proper names or quotations.

PROLOGUE

Mary O'Donnell sat in a corner booth in a small pub in Belfast, waiting for her lunch of shepherd's pie. Her head hurt after a long month of talking with women and activists in Belfast. Mary is a member of the Northern Ireland Women's Coalition (NIWC) and had been engaged in surveying women about conditions in Northern Ireland as the NIWC leaders prepared to reengage in the multiparty talks at Stormont (the common name for the buildings that held the government of Northern Ireland) that had been convened by British prime minister John Major in 1996 and now were being restarted in June 1997 by the new prime minister, Tony Blair. In order to help the two NIWC representatives at the talks, she and other women had been reaching out across Northern Ireland to seek out the voices of women, clergy, and cross-community activists, both Catholic and Protestant, Unionist and Nationalist, working class and middle class. She was struck again and again by the divisions that existed between the two cultural communities and the walls of segregation in education, housing, and employment that kept each side from having direct experience of the other.

To get women to talk with her, she first had to overcome their initial deep suspicions, rooted in a society that had been at war for thirty years and in which, no matter what street you lived on, you experienced the surveillance of the police (the Royal Ulster Constabulary [RUC]), the British army (which had now patrolled the streets for over twenty-five years), and the local paramilitaries—the Republican Provisional Irish Republican Army (IRA) or the Loyalist Ulster Volunteer Force (UVF), Ulster Freedom Fighters (UFF), and Ulster Defence Association (UDA). Any person she talked to immediately wanted to know what community she was from so that they would know how to shade their comments based on whether she was an enemy or a friend. If you admitted to being from East Belfast or West Belfast, you were immediately pegged as Protestant or Catholic. If your last name was Johnson, Hunter, Robinson, or Prescott, you were seen as Protestant and presumed to be a Unionist who wanted Northern Ireland to remain as part of the United Kingdom (also known as Great Britain); if it was Sullivan, Murphy, Collins, or yes, O'Donnell, then you were Catholic and presumed to be a Nationalist who wanted to leave the United Kingdom and become part of the Republic of Ireland. With over 98 percent of students attending segregated secondary schools, just the name of the school you or your children attended tipped off your religion. There was a lack of regular interaction among most Protestants and Catholics driven apart by a long history of discrimination and now thirty years of sectarian bloodshed in which 3,600 people had died, thousands more been injured, and nearly every family touched by the death or imprisonment of family members. It was very difficult to establish trust and open communication with members of either community.

Mary was deeply moved by heart-breaking stories from all sides. She put down the pen with which she made notes and let her mind travel back to those hard conversations. She recalled the emotions:

Fear: she met with women who had no idea that their husbands or sons were in a paramilitary group until they were suddenly arrested or interned. Or worse for one woman, who had two masked men come to the door and warn her that if her son did not stop his activities, he would be subject to their brand of justice—shooting him in both knees (a practice common to the paramilitary groups on both sides, who used it to stop "antisocial behavior" within their respective communities). She arranged for her son to go live with her sister in London to escape. For others it was fear as their children went about their daily rounds in the city. One mother lost her son when he was one of three civilians gunned down outside his place of work, even though he belonged to no political organization. Another mother lost her daughter after she and her friends went joyriding—when they came upon a British patrol and she and her boyfriend were shot to death. Another woman only learned her husband was a member of the UVF when he was briefly arrested and then released by the RUC. But having once been arrested he was then known to the IRA, who rolled past their house in a car and shot fifteen bullets into him as he walked out of his house to go to the corner and buy cigarettes. For many there was a basic fear because they did not know when or why sudden violence might strike their families. And if it did happen, they experienced deep disappointment that often there could be no justice for many of the victims. No one would ever be prosecuted or explain why a precious daughter or son had been killed.

Pride and Dedication: for many, however, there was a dedication to their community and a pride in the men and women who were fighting to defend it. One woman bragged that "she was British and proud of it!" She was an Ulster Protestant and an Ulster Loyalist who had been raised in the Shankhill neighborhood in Belfast by a father who had fought for the king in the British army. When a close friend was shot dead by the IRA, she found out at the funeral that he had been a member of the UVF and that her husband was a member too. But she was proud that they defended their own people from terrorists, and that the Unionists as a whole had the courage to stand up to the Catholic Church and its control of thought in the Irish Republic. To her mind the people of Ulster were British, and the people of Ireland were Irish and never would they be able to come together.

Another woman spoke of her husband as a proud IRA freedom fighter determined to seize independence from Britain. Violence was necessary because the British gave them no option. They believed that violence had proved to work in Cyprus, Malta, Rhodesia, and Kenya, where the British colonizers at first insisted that they would never sit down with terrorists but in the end were forced to negotiate with their opponents to end the British imperial control of those states. Only the IRA, in her opinion, was willing to try to improve conditions for Catholics and to defend their neighborhoods from Unionist attacks.

One university teacher spoke of being Irish as something that you are born and socialized into, by your parents (his father was an ardent Nationalist), by your school, by your reading of the past, by love of Irish culture and literature, by the football team that you follow, by the presence of the British army which subjects you to checkpoints and searches and makes you feel like a refugee without rights in your own country. If, he argued, there is no other way to be heard, then violence is inevitable and acceptable until the British are driven out. And then the Protestants and Catholics could negotiate their own future in conversation with the Republic of Ireland.

Anger and Revenge: one Catholic priest had tried to explain to her that the churches, both Catholic and Protestant, and the British government had failed to give disillusioned young people any alternative to violence. Raised in sectarian households, knowing little of the other community, they were trapped in unemployment and brutalized by repressive police. They felt justified in using violence to try to bring about change or to get revenge because the system gave them no nonviolent outlet for their disillusionment and frustration. History, the priest claimed, is what separated the two communities most. He emphasized the British oppression of the Irish peoples for hundreds of years, which made the Republicans that he visited in prison see themselves as freedom fighters connected to the heroes of the Easter Rising of 1916 and beyond. The British had treated them as subhuman, and if the anger and resentment sometimes led to the brutal killings of civilians in bombings and revenge shootings, it was to be regretted; but they believed there was no alternative other than to put pressure on the British army and government to leave Ireland.

A Presbyterian minister laid the blame for the divisions in society at the feet of the Roman Catholic Church which insisted that Catholic children only attend Catholic schools, as well as the Republic of Ireland which insisted on maintaining a claim to Northern Ireland in its constitution, even though the majority of people in Northern Ireland clearly wanted to be part of Great Britain with the English, Scotch, and Welsh. He blamed the IRA for turning to violence because it could not succeed in convincing people to leave the United Kingdom. He saw the Sinn Féin party as no more than a political front for terrorists. The IRA/Sinn Féin could not expect any legitimacy until they categorically rejected the use of violence and gave up their weapons.

From each community she heard again and again that their violence was justified by the violence of the other side—protecting their community or getting revenge for the killing of civilians. Many Protestants were willing to grant that rules on housing and employment needed to become fairer; but who was concerned that many of the Protestants also had no jobs or lived in poor housing? And don't they have a higher standard of living in the North than in the South? As one woman put it, her grandfather had been killed on the Somme in 1916 fighting for Britain, her father had been wounded in North Africa in World War II fighting for Britain, where was the British recognition of their loyalty? Where was respect for the sacrifices that they had made? Why couldn't the Catholics accept that the majority of the people in Northern Ireland were British? What was the point of trying to have a dialogue with people who were determined to destroy the state?

One Loyalist woman frankly said, "I have nothing against Catholics. If that is their religion let them practice it . . . south of the border."[1] Ulster, she claimed was part of the United Kingdom, and her ancestors had fought for 400 years to keep it that way. She was brought up to believe that the Twelfth of July was the greatest day of the year, when they celebrated ancient Protestant victories with parades and marches.

Hope: Mary also sensed something else in many of the people with whom she spoke. It was a recognition that things had to change, and dare she say it, many even expressed cautious hope. There were small interdenominational schools in which Catholic and Protestant students could study together the main events of the past such as the Battle of the Boyne in 1690 or the Easter Rising in 1916 and come to some understanding of how these events were interpreted differently by each community. Even as the students retained a strong sense of their own sectarian identity, they could come to understand the strong sense of identity held by the other community as well and begin to see that the solution was not violence but some form of tolerance and compromise. Far too few students got to mix socially with those of a different upbringing, however, but cross-community groups were pushing to establish more opportunities for interaction and communication within any agreement.

There was hope in the growing community activism that reached out to help victims of violence or agitated for peace. It had started with the Peace People led by Mairead Corrigan, Betty Williams, and Ciara McKeown in the 1970s and led eventually to the formation of the NIWC in the 1990s. Mary had talked to leaders of groups like the Families against Intimidation and Terror (FAIT), formed by Nancy Gracey after her son was shot in the kneecaps by the IRA. The FAIT brought attention to the human costs of the conflict and campaigned to stop the brutal mutilation campaigns that paramilitaries inflicted on both sides. Tied to that hope of ending violence was a sense of shame expressed by some who were ardent Nationalists: shame that even if war was justified against the British army, it did not justify actions that killed innocent civilians, such as the Enniskillen bombing at a Remembrance Day celebration in November 1987 that left 11 civilians dead. In that sense of shame was a dawning recognition that they needed to turn to peaceful means to solve their problems.

More people were becoming frustrated with how religious sectarianism seemed to block any real progress on basic issues, such as poverty or women's rights. One woman she talked to worked at a women's advice center that counseled both Catholic and Protestant women. She noted that many who came in to ask for her help never asked about her religious affiliation. They realized that women had problems in common, whether it was access to birth control, options for unwanted pregnancies, dealing with an abusive spouse, or trying to provide for and protect their families. They were women first and Protestant or Catholic, Nationalist or Unionist second.

Mary tried to understand. Couldn't more people be made to see that any settlement to end the Troubles would allow their society to improve the quality of all people's lives, whatever the community in which they were born? How could the working classes ever improve their lot if they spent so much of their energy in fear and anger and frustration at the wasted lives of children caught up in continued sectarian war? Could the party leaders find a political solution that protected the identity of each community and yet brought them to work together on common problems?

New leaders in Britain and Ireland gave hope. Paramilitary groups' willingness to declare ceasefires so that politicians could negotiate gave hope. The fact that both the Republic of Ireland and Great Britain had joined the European Union offered a forum to debate ideas about the free movement of people and goods and a universal statement of human rights that could provide the guideposts to end religious discrimination. Indeed, the visit of the American president Bill Clinton in 1995, carefully orchestrated to show respect to both communities, also demonstrated that the outside world, which seemed to have ignored the problems of Northern Ireland for so long, was now willing to help them achieve a lasting peace.

Mary sighed and took a sip of her pint. She picked up her pen once again, trying to write a report that could recognize the pain but also provide support for the hope that so many people in Northern Ireland expressed. Were the majority now ready to end the violence and take the risk of peace? But she was also realistic and recognized that the major parties were still far apart in their visions for Northern Ireland. It would be difficult to get the long-time enemies to talk with each other around the same conference table, let alone come to a political solution to the crisis. Moreover, she realized that any violent event—a massive bombing, the assassination of a key leader—would render it that much more difficult to persuade the two communities to recognize each other's cultural pride and to give up their fears, angers, frustrations, and desires for revenge. Could the parties meeting at Stormont possibly find a peace that respected the rights of both communities and lead them to work together within the same political framework? Or were they doomed to more years of violence?

BASIC FEATURES OF REACTING TO THE PAST

This is a historical role-playing game set in a moment of heightened historical tension; it places you in the role of a person from the period. After a few preparatory lectures, the game begins and the students are in charge. By reading the game book and your individual role sheet, you will find out more about your objectives, worldview, allies, and opponents. You must then attempt to achieve victory through formal speeches, informal debate, negotiations, and conspiracy. Outcomes sometimes differ from actual history; a debriefing session sets the record straight. What follows is an outline of what you will encounter in Reacting and what you will be expected to do.

Game Setup

Your instructor will spend some time before the beginning of the game helping you to understand the historical context for the game. During the setup period, you will use several different kinds of material:

- The game book (what you are reading now), which includes historical information, rules and elements of the game, and essential historical documents.
- A role sheet, which provides a short biography of the historical person you will model in the game as well as that person's ideology, objectives, responsibilities, and resources. Some roles are based on historical figures. Others are "composites," with elements drawn from a number of individuals. You will receive your role sheet from your instructor.

Familiarize yourself with the documents before the game begins and return to them once you are in role. They contain information and arguments that will be useful as the game unfolds. A second reading while *in role* will deepen your understanding and alter your perspective. Once the game is in motion, your perspectives may change. Some ideas may begin to look quite different. Those who have carefully read the materials and who know the rules of the game will invariably do better than those who rely on general impressions and uncertain memories.

Game Play

Once the game begins, class sessions are run by students. In most cases, a single student serves as a sort of presiding officer. The instructor then becomes the "game master" or "game manager" (GM) and takes a seat in the back of the room. Though they do not lead the class sessions, GMs may do any of the following:

- Pass notes
- Announce important events
- Redirect proceedings that have gone off track

Instructors are, of course, available for consultations before and after game sessions. Although they will not let you in on any of the secrets of the game, they can be invaluable in terms of sharpening your arguments or finding key historical resources.

The presiding officer is expected to observe basic standards of fairness, but as a fail-safe device, most games employ the "podium rule," which allows a student who has not been recognized to approach the podium and wait for a chance to speak. Once at the podium, the student has the floor and must be heard.

Role sheets contain private, secret information that you must guard. Exercise caution when discussing your role with others. Your role sheet might identify likely allies, but even they may not always be trustworthy. However, keeping your own counsel and saying nothing to anyone is not an option. To achieve your objectives, you *must* speak with others. You will never muster the voting strength to prevail without allies. Collaboration and coalition building are at the heart of every game.

Some games feature strong alliances called *factions*. As a counterbalance, these games include roles called *indeterminates*. They operate outside the established factions, and while some are entirely neutral, most possess their own idiosyncratic objectives. If you are in a faction, cultivating indeterminates is in your interest, since they can be persuaded to support your position. If you are lucky enough to have drawn the role of an indeterminate, you should be pleased: you will likely play a pivotal role in the outcome of the game.

Game Requirements

Students playing Reacting games practice persuasive writing, public speaking, critical thinking, teamwork, negotiation, problem solving, collaboration, adapting to changing circumstances, and working under pressure to meet deadlines. Your instructor will explain the specific requirements for your class. In general, though, a Reacting game asks you to perform three distinct activities:

Reading and writing. What you read can often be put to immediate use, and what you write is meant to persuade others to act the way you want them to. The reading load may vary slightly from role to role, and the writing requirement depends on your particular course. Papers are often policy statements, but they can also be autobiographies, battle plans, newspaper articles, poems, or after-game reflections. Papers often provide the foundation for the speeches delivered in class. They also help to familiarize you with the issues, which should allow you to ask good questions.

Public speaking and debate. In the course of a game, almost everyone is expected to deliver at least one formal speech from the podium (the length of the game and the size of the class will determine the number of speeches). Debate follows. It can be impromptu, raucous, and fast-paced. At some point, discussions must lead to action, which often means proposing, debating, and passing a variety of resolutions. GMs may stipulate that students deliver their papers from memory when at the podium, or they may insist that students begin to wean themselves from dependency on written notes as the game progresses.

Wherever the game imaginatively puts you, it will surely not put you in the present. Accordingly, the colloquialisms and familiarities of today's college life are out of place. Never open your speech with a salutation like "Hi guys" when something like "Fellow citizens!" would be more appropriate.

Always seek allies to back up your points when you are speaking at the podium. Do your best to have at least one supporter second your proposal, come to your defense, or admonish inattentive members of the body. Note-passing and side conversations, while common occurrences, will likely spoil the effect of your speech; so you and your supporters should insist on order before such behavior becomes too disruptive. Ask the presiding officer to assist you. Appeal to the GM as a last resort.

Strategizing. Communication among students is an essential feature of Reacting games. You will likely find yourself writing emails, texting, attending out-of-class meetings, or gathering for meals. The purpose of frequent communication is to lay out a strategy for achieving your objectives, thwarting your opponents, and hatching plots. When communicating with fellow students in or out of class, always assume that they are speaking to you in role. If you want to talk about the "real world," make that clear.

Controversy

This game deals with events and issues that can spark powerful emotions and reactions. The Troubles not only stirred political debates but also opened up deep wounds of hatred and emotional trauma among perpetrators and victims. Almost every participant in the talks has felt the impact of the violence on themselves, their families, and/or their friends. Derogatory stereotypes and ethnic slurs were part of everyday language. Protestants might call Catholics "Taigs" or "Fenians." Hardliners might also use biblical language to condemn the Catholic Church and "Papists" —read the language that Ian Paisley uses in his speech to the Democratic Unionist Party's annual conference (core text no. 21). Catholics might refer to Protestants as "Prods," or employ anticolonial language to condemn their British oppressors. Your GM will discuss with the class the kinds of language that might arise in the sources and help students to determine what is acceptable.

It is your task in a role-playing game to immerse yourself in the identity of your role and embody your character without caricature. But students in the midst of a debate may find themselves using language or raising their voices in ways that would not be appropriate in a normal classroom. Urgency, frustrations, and even anger may be part of the emotions that occur among students. It will be important to remember two things. First, as you attempt to rationally persuade the other students of what is best for the future of Northern Ireland, it may be appropriate at times to evoke emotions, employ stereotypes to appeal to your constituents, or to display strong feelings without using overly offensive language. Second, it is important that you always remember that these emotions and stereotypes are directed at the role being played by another student and not at the student personally. Always be careful to separate what is appropriate for your role from your normal relationships with other students. In discussing the use of the language in the game, the GM will make students aware of the historical basis of common stereotypes, set ground rules for the debates, and deal with concerns that arise during the course of play. They may call your attention to words or activities that cross the line between role-playing and personal attacks during the debates.

Counterfactuals

In the actual peace talks, the Democratic Unionist Party (DUP), the United Kingdom Unionist Party (UKUP), and Sinn Féin were never in the room at the same time. Since it is important for ideas from all of these parties to be part of the debate, if Sinn Féin is readmitted to the talks after the decommissioning discussion, the DUP and UKUP cannot choose to walk out of the talks until the start of the third meeting of the talks. They will remain in the room with Sinn Féin during the initial debates over the constitutional and Strand 1 issues.

2

Historical Background

CHRONOLOGY

1912 Ulster Unionists led by Edward Carson form the Ulster Volunteer Force to oppose Home Rule. Five hundred thousand men and women sign the Ulster Covenant pledging to defend the Union.

1916 The Easter Rising in Dublin, although quicky defeated, enables IRA rebels to proclaim the Irish Republic.

1919 Sinn Féin members of Parliament refuse to take their seats in the British Parliament and instead constitute themselves the Irish National Assembly, the Dáil Éireann. The Anglo-Irish War begins.

1921 The British divide the six northern counties from the South and hold an election of the first Northern Ireland Assembly.

1922–23 The Anglo-Irish Treaty recognizes the division of Ireland—Northern Ireland (six counties of Ulster) remains in the United Kingdom, the rest becomes the Irish Free State, with dominion status in the British Empire. For the next fifty years the government of Northern Ireland is dominated by the Ulster Unionist Party (UUP).

1968 The Northern Irish Catholic minority launches a civil rights campaign to demand civil rights from the Protestant government. Riots follow.

1969 January: Civil rights marchers are attacked by Loyalists at Burntollet Bridge near Derry/Londonderry. August: Battle of the Bogside in Derry/Londonderry. Protestants burn out Catholic homes in Belfast. The British army is deployed in Northern Ireland to keep the peace. December: The IRA splits, creating the Provisional IRA committed to war against Great Britain. (The Provisional IRA will be referred to as the IRA in this text.)

1970 Five hundred Nationalist workers are expelled from the shipyards in Belfast. The Social Democratic and Labour Party (SDLP) is formed.

1971 Internment without trial is introduced, initially 450 Catholics are arrested and interrogated, although eventually some Protestant Loyalists are also interned. Ian Paisley founds the Democratic Unionist Party. Protestant paramilitary groups, the Ulster Volunteer Force (UVF) and the Ulster Defence Association (UDA), launch a campaign of sectarian assassinations.

1972 British troops kill 13 Catholic protesters on "Bloody Sunday" in Derry/Londonderry (1 more dies later in hospital for a total of 14). In retaliation IRA car bombs kill 11 and injure 130 in Belfast ("Bloody Friday"). The British government suspends Protestant-dominated administration (Stormont) in Belfast and introduces direct rule. In 1972, 470 people (police, British army, paramilitaries, and civilians) are killed and 4,876 injured as a result of the Troubles.

1974 Britain implements plans for a new Northern Irish assembly in the Sunningdale Agreement. This new executive collapses in May after strikes by Unionist workers protesting against power-sharing. Direct rule resumes. Thirty-three people are killed by car bombs in the Irish Republic. Twenty-one people are killed in an IRA bombing of two Birmingham, England pubs.

1977 The organizers of the Ulster Peace Movement, Mairead Corrigan and Betty Williams, are awarded the Nobel Peace Prize, but their movement fails to lead to a broader settlement.

1979 IRA steps up attacks on prominent Britons, killing the ambassador to the Netherlands, Sir Richard Sykes; Conservative Party spokesman on Northern Ireland Airey Neave; and Lord Mountbatten, cousin of Queen Elizabeth, in separate incidents. Eleven members of the Shankhill Butchers, a Loyalist gang, are convicted of nineteen murders.

1981 Ten IRA prisoners, starting with Bobby Sands, starve to death in hunger strikes designed to secure political prisoner status. Sinn Féin uses the strikers' popularity to stand candidates for election to the British Parliament, Sands was elected one month before his death.

1982 IRA bombs in London kill eleven soldiers. The Irish National Liberation Army bombs a Ballykelly pub, killing eleven soldiers and six civilians. A new Northern Ireland assembly is elected but boycotted by Catholics.

1983 An IRA bomb at Harrod's department store in London kills six and injures ninety.

1984 An IRA bomb at a British Conservative Party conference kills five. Prime Minister Margaret Thatcher escapes injury.

1985 The Anglo-Irish Agreement gives the Dublin government a consultative voice in the daily running of Northern Ireland, prompting 100,000 Unionists to attend a demonstration against the agreement in Belfast.

1987 Eight IRA gunmen are killed in ambush by British Special Air Service Regiment soldiers. An IRA bomb kills eleven at an Enniskillen war memorial ceremony.

1988 Three unarmed members of an IRA active service unit are shot dead by British troops in Gibraltar. IRA bombs kill six soldiers in Lisburn and eight in Tyrone.

1989 Ten British army bandsmen are killed in IRA bomb at a Royal Marines music school in southern England.

1990 John Major replaces Margaret Thatcher as leader of the Conservative Party and prime minister of Great Britain.

1991 An IRA mortar attack on 10 Downing Street results in no casualties. Secret talks begin between the SDLP's John Hume and Sinn Féin's Gerry Adams and between the British government and Sinn Féin.

1992 Five Catholics are killed by a Loyalist gunman in a bookmaker's shop in Belfast. An IRA car bomb in City of London financial district kills three and injures ninety-one.

1993 IRA bombs in the English town of Warrington and in central London kill three people. IRA bombs a fish shop in the Protestant part of Belfast, killing nine. The Protestant Ulster Freedom Fighters kill seven Catholics at a pub in Greysteel in revenge. The Anglo-Irish Downing Street Declaration is issued in December; Britain says it would not block an end to British rule if a majority wanted it and offers Sinn Féin a seat at peace talks if IRA violence ends.

1994 The IRA announces ceasefire in August, with Loyalist groups following suit in October. British officials hold the first open meeting with Sinn Féin in more than seventy years.

1995 US president Bill Clinton visits Northern Ireland.

1996 A commission headed by former US senator George Mitchell proposes political talks alongside a phased surrender of guerrilla weapons. The IRA abandons its ceasefire and bombs Canary Wharf in London, killing 2 people and injuring 100. John Major initiates multiparty talks on the future of Northern Ireland at Stormont in Belfast in June, but Sinn Féin is excluded because of IRA violence. The IRA explodes a bomb in a Manchester shopping center, injuring 200.

1997 Tony Blair succeeds Major as British prime minister in May with a solid Labour Party majority in Parliament and reengages the government in the multiparty talks. Talks resume on 3 June.

OVERVIEW OF THE TROUBLES

Ending the Troubles focuses on the efforts to end thirty years of violence in Northern Ireland known as "the Troubles." The conflict pitted two communities against one another, each with different concepts of its national culture, identity, and political allegiances. To begin to grapple with the essential divisions and problems faced by decision-makers in 1997 and 1998, it is important to examine the history of Ireland and understand its relationship to England (also referred to as Great Britain and the United Kingdom) as well as the relationships on the island between the native Irish and later English and Scottish settlers. It is also important to understand basic concepts of nationalism in order to comprehend the political options that were open to the Irish communities. Why did narrower concepts of distinct national communities have more success in Ireland than broader views of a more cosmopolitan state? What opportunity did the Irish have in the 1990s to build connections between varying concepts of nationalism and bring together their historically distinct and warring political and cultural movements?

Chapter 2, "Historical Background," is divided into three sections: the first focuses on the deep roots of the conflict in an overview of 1,000 years of Irish history; the second focuses on the twentieth-century history of Northern Ireland; the third on the Troubles. Students and instructors who wish to examine the theoretical debates over nationalism can consult works listed in the bibliography.

National identity can be depicted as an imagined community in which we identify with a larger group most of whose members we don't know personally, but that serves to help define our personal identity as distinct from other groups. For much of Europe's early history, a sense of *national consciousness*—of being Irish, or English or Welsh or Scottish or French or Basque or Czech—was based on living in a common geographic area, having a common culture (religion, art, folk traditions, etc.), a common language, and common historical experiences (of wars, plagues, natural disasters, etc.). But governmental

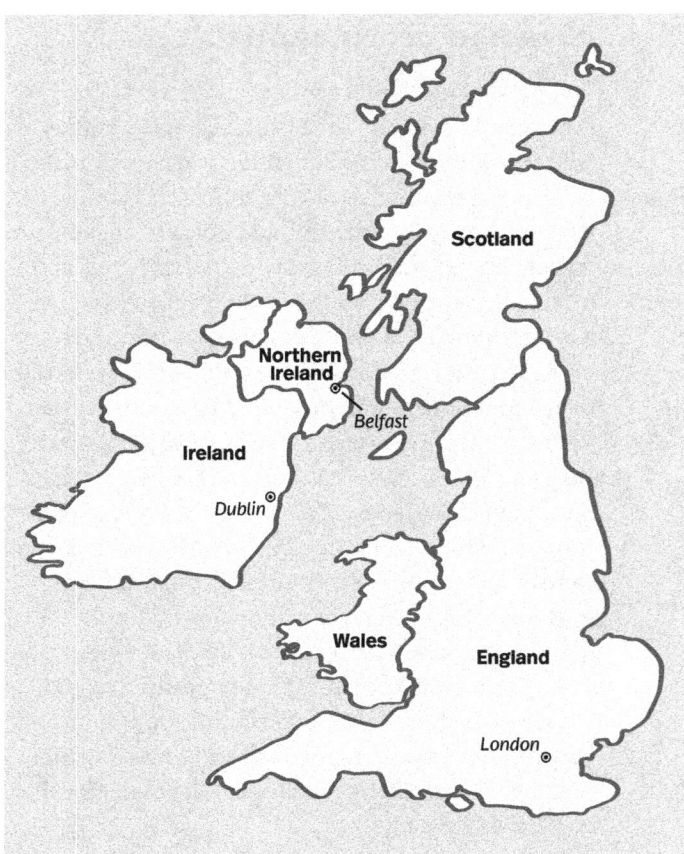

The British Isles

organization was not based on these national identities. Instead, political loyalty was founded on feudal obligations and personal oaths of loyalty based on marriage alliances, conquests, and kinship among the landed elite. People of different classes, orders, and religions held unequal rights and privileges based on their rank within this hierarchical society. Commonly people with different national identities existed side-by-side within the larger state of a monarch or emperor, particularly as European powers centralized their authority by the seventeenth century using a combination of divine right theory, social persuasion, and military force. Thus, Ireland found itself drawn under the authority of English monarchs through a combination of political alliances, marriages, conquest, and the suppression of rebellions.

Nationalism became a more potent and more aggressive ideology in the eighteenth and nineteenth centuries when the earlier, looser sense of national consciousness became tied to revolutionary movements in the American and French Revolutions. For our purposes in understanding Irish history, it will be useful to use broad distinctions between *Civic or political nationalism* and *cultural nationalism*, drawn from the works of John Hutchinson and of John McGarry and Brendan O'Leary that are listed in the bibliography.

Civic nationalism has as its object the making of a secular, representative state that will guarantee its members equal political rights within a government based on popular sovereignty. The citizens participate in making the laws (or selecting representatives who make the laws). National identity is a matter of choice, in which citizens choose the state in which they live and give their allegiance. This secular liberal

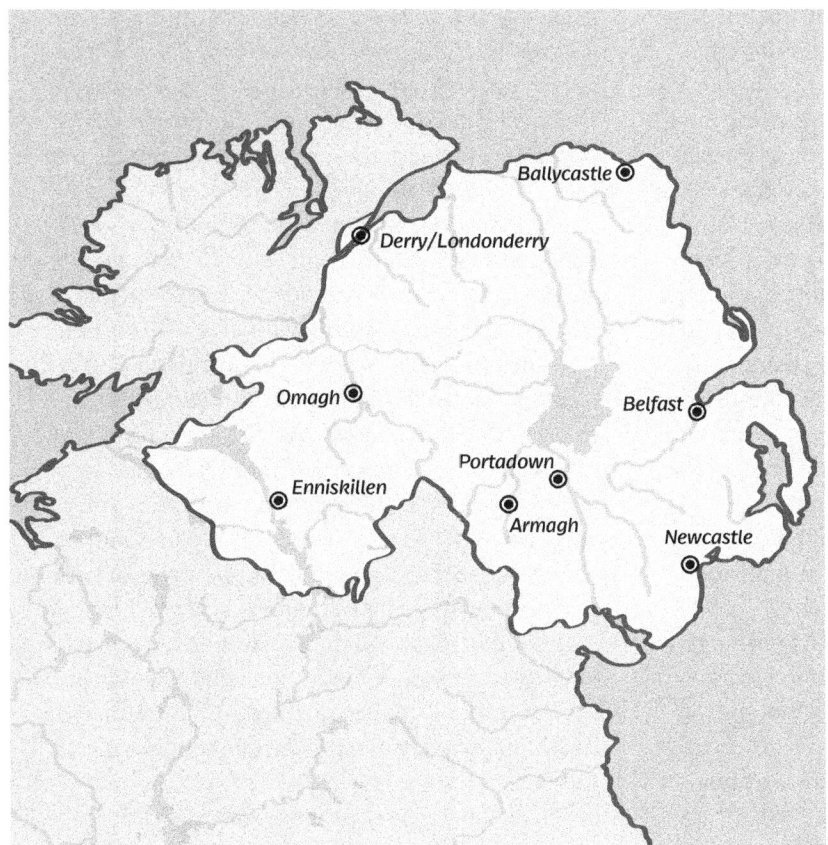

Northern Ireland

ideology imagined a state where the basic liberties of free speech, press, religion, and due process of law were promised to every citizen whatever their social standing or religious belief. The larger hopes of those who combined liberal concepts of civic and national identity was that a world in which each nation organized its own government based on popular sovereignty and equality of rights would be able to exist in peace. They placed an initial emphasis on developing constitutions that limited government powers to protecting the liberty of the individual citizens to pursue their own rights and interests. Unfortunately, the wars of the French Revolution and Napoleonic era and the conservative backlash against liberal democracy in the nineteenth century proved that the ideal of the civic nationalists would be difficult to achieve. Still, this type of liberal political nationalism would find echoes in Ireland in the revolt of the United Irishmen in 1798, in the hopes of both Protestant and Catholic politicians who fought for Home Rule for Ireland in the late nineteenth century, and even in the original concepts of a secular republic among some nationalist revolutionaries (see below).

Cultural nationalism developed in the nineteenth and twentieth centuries: inspired by the examples of the French Revolution and spurred by nineteenth-century Romanticism. Cultural nationalism does not primarily seek to establish a state that provides a broad umbrella of equal rights for autonomous citizens. Instead, it focuses on the nation as a historical and moral community with a distinct identity from other ethnic and cultural groups. Instead of a matter of political choice, a person's national identity is determined by their birth and inheritance of an ethnic tradition. Writers and politicians who pursued a cultural nationalism sought to play upon a sense of national consciousness by reviving the historical traditions, cultural practices, and the spirit of the religion of their ancient cultural community in order to achieve a moral regeneration of the nation. Intellectuals played a large role in revivifying dying languages (such as Irish) and arts, looking for heroes and moral models in ancient and medieval history (such as stories of the legendary hero Cuchulainn in Ireland) that were unique to their ethnic or national group, and then used the people's traditions to establish a spiritual and moral ideal for the nation. Individuals were seen as dependent on the national culture for their own identity and even survival and were urged to be faithful to the point of being willing to sacrifice their own lives for the nation.

Joining national cultural identity to the revolutionary concept of popular sovereignty made for a powerful force in modern European history, as each ethnic group began to celebrate its uniqueness, reject foreign influences, and insist on its right to self-governance in an independent nation-state in competition against competing national groups. Ultimately, the push for national self-determination by the larger ethnic groups helped lead to the collapse of the great European empires after they were exhausted on the battlefields of World War I. But the hope of a new era of peaceful democracy after 1918 was shattered when fascists movements proved able to turn many of the elements of cultural nationalism into more racist and violent movements in the 1920s and 1930s. Much of European history after the tragedy of World War I has been an effort to find a balance between international cooperation to establish universal rights and to promote economic prosperity, on the one hand, and the continued existence of narrower cultural concepts of national sovereignty, on the other.

The interplay of culture, religion, politics, and national identity is more complex than can be captured in a simple summary. But as representatives of political parties in Northern Ireland in the 1990s, you will need to be acutely aware of the development of different concepts of national identity in Irish history and the events, heroes, and institutions by which each national community defines its unique identity and rights. *Use the broad concepts of national consciousness, civic nationalism, and cultural nationalism to help make sense of the evolution of political conflict in Northern Ireland and to understand why two competing communities evolve on the island— one that looks for its identity to the native Irish (also referred to as Gaelic or Celtic) and Catholic traditions as well as to a history of republican political rebellion to forge a concept of a united Ireland, and the other that gives its allegiance to Great Britain and looks to a culture rooted in the defense of Protestantism and constitutional monarchy.* Can you as representatives in the multiparty talks at Stormont in Belfast in 1997 and 1998 give voice to the nationalist aspirations of your own party as well as strive to understand the historical roots of the competing concepts of national community in Northern Ireland? Will you insist on maintaining those separate identities? Or will you identify processes or institutions that might bring each community to accept the other in a united Ireland or in a devolved government in Northern Ireland?

You are facing not just the ideological differences between parties but the lived experience of thirty years of sectarian conflict. Between 1968 and 1998 more than 3,600 people were killed and thousands more injured in the violence of "the Troubles." Non-Irish observers may have some sense of religious differences being part of the problem but often have little understanding that the conflict also had cultural, economic, and political sources that go beyond any theological differences. Two cultural communities, two nationalisms, existed side-by-side in competition for land, housing, jobs, education, and political power. The widening number of victims deepened many of the hatreds, creating desires for revenge and justifying the use of violence by each side to protect its community. To the outside world the Irish, Scots, Welsh, and English all seem part of the same ethnicity and certainly their descendants live side-by-side in the United States without antagonism. But the ethnic and nationalist divisions in Northern Ireland run deep, and to understand them and the difficult problems faced by those who wanted to bridge those divides during the 1990s requires a basic understanding of Irish history.

It is important to understand some terms. If you believe that the people of Northern Ireland are British citizens and should remain in the United Kingdom, you are a **Unionist**, probably a **Protestant,** and your paramilitary groups may be referred to as **Loyalists**; you call your homeland **Ulster**.

Unionists are committed to retaining Northern Ireland within the United Kingdom. They are mainly **Protestants**, either Anglican (Church of England/Ireland, acknowledging the British monarch as the head of the church) or Presbyterian. **Loyalists** are hardline **Unionists** who are willing to use violence to achieve their goals and often participate in paramilitary groups such as the **Ulster** Volunteer Force (UVF), the Ulster Freedom Fighters (UFF), or the Ulster Defence Association (UDA).

If you believe that the United Kingdom should surrender its control of Northern Ireland in order to reunite all thirty-two counties of the island of Ireland, then you are a **Nationalist**, probably a **Catholic**, and your paramilitary groups refer to themselves as **Republican**; you prefer to refer to the six counties in Ulster as the North.

Nationalists are committed to reuniting the six counties of Northern Ireland with the twenty-six counties of the Republic of Ireland. They are mainly **Roman Catholics** who acknowledge the religious authority of the bishop of Rome, the pope. **Republicans** are hardline Nationalists who are willing to use violence to achieve their goals and often participate in paramilitary groups such as the Irish Republican Army (IRA).

Both traditions believe that they have been mistreated by Britain (in different ways) and can call upon a history that validates resistance, the use of violence, and personal self-sacrifice for the greater cause. They can clearly identify their own kin and their enemies by the street they live on, the sports they play, and even the names they bear. An Ian, Grace, or William would most likely be a Protestant; a Sean, Seamus, or Theresa would most likely be Catholic. All have a critical stake in how national identities were formed and defended in Ireland's troubled history.

THE ENGLISH IN IRELAND

The Origins of the English in Ireland

In the early centuries of the Common Era (a secular term to designate the time after the birth of Jesus Christ), Ireland was a rough land, difficult to control because its geography of mountains, lakes, and bogs divided the natives into some 150 Celtic tribes, each with their own king, fighting for land and power. A high king of Ireland could be designated, but these monarchs often spent their reign in warfare trying to enforce their authority over competing families—the most famous being Brian Boru, who died in battle in 1014. These Celtic tribes never achieved a centralized state. Saint Patrick and other churchmen brought Roman Catholic Christianity to the island in the 400s and started a strong monastic tradition that was key to preserving ancient learning when the Roman Empire fell to the barbarians, but the internal competition for power continued in Ireland.[1] That disunity was an opportunity for invaders such as the Danish (Vikings) who attacked in the ninth and tenth centuries, at times invited in as allies by various Irish families. Their fortified camps led to the founding of future cities, such as Dublin, Cork, Limerick, and Wexford, where over time the Vikings intermarried with the native Irish.

By the twelfth century, at a time when all Europe was under the religious domination of the Roman Catholic Church, Pope Adrian IV issued a bull in 1155 empowering King Henry II of England to conquer Ireland. He cited Henry's "pious and laudable desire" to bring order to Ireland "for the enlargement of the bounds of the church, for the restraint of vice, for the correction of morals and the introduction of virtues, for the advancement of the Christian religion."[2] The pope was interested in exercising doctrinal control over the independent Irish church and in gaining "the annual pension of one penny from each house" to be sent to Rome. Henry II (who also controlled half of France) was interested in expanding his own power, finding land and estates to reward his Anglo-Norman nobles, and ensuring that Ireland could not become a base for his enemies. In later years, when England's power became more dependent on the sea, its navy, and its colonies, English monarchs became even more determined to make sure that Ireland did not threaten England's back door by falling to the Spanish or French or Germans.

The Anglo-Norman noble Strongbow, invited over by the deposed Irish king of Leinster, who was seeking English aid to defeat his rivals, led the first English invasion of Ireland in 1170, followed by Henry II himself two years later. But Henry could only subdue about half of Ireland before being distracted by wars in France, and subsequent years witnessed a competition for power between Irish and English nobles. The English (as we will refer to these Anglo-Norman invaders) established their administrative center in the city of Dublin, built castles and cathedrals, imposed the English legal system, and even created an Irish parliament in 1297—under the control of the English king, of course. The Crown regularly suppressed rebellions of Ireland's native landed gentry and was concerned that marriage alliances between some of the first Anglo-Norman families and the Irish were blurring identities and loyalties. In fact, through marriage over time many of these Anglo-Normans became so thoroughly Irish in blood and culture that by the seventeenth century Protestants would have regarded them as Irish. To maintain the distinction between the English rulers and the native Irish population, the Crown issued the Statues of Kilkenny in 1366, prohibiting marriage between the English and Irish, as well as forbidding the use of the Irish language, fashions, or names by the English settlers. At this point there was a strong sense of national consciousness that led the English to look upon the native Irish as a colonized people, but political loyalty was still largely dependent on feudal and personal ties.

English efforts to exert centralized control over Ireland and to establish a strong barrier between the Irish and English nationalities became more intense because of the Protestant Reformation (a revolt against the power and doctrine of the Roman Catholic Church and the pope, see the discussion of religion in chapter 3, "The Game."). When King Henry

English and Scottish Plantations of Ireland, 1620

Areas that were taken from the native Irish in the sixteenth and seventeenth centuries

VIII broke with Rome and Parliament proclaimed him head of the Church of England in the 1530s, it added a new religious angle to the political conflicts over England's domination of Ireland. In 1541 Henry also established the Church of Ireland, headed by himself as the king (thus the Anglican Church has two branches, both under the English monarch—the Church of England and the Church of Ireland), eventually dividing the English landlords in Ireland, who became Anglican, from the mass of native Irish, who remained overwhelmingly Catholic. Remaining Catholic was not seen as a benign religious choice. It meant defying the authority of the king by continuing to believe in the authority of the pope. When the monarch claimed that royal power derived from God by divine right, anyone who did not practice the same religion was questioning that royal authority and could be branded a traitor.[3]

Irish Catholic nobles rebelled against England in the 1530s and the 1580s. The response of English kings and queens was not only military action and political repression but also a move to suppress what was seen as the inferior and treasonous culture of the Irish in order to make the population more loyal to the Crown. In a series of actions known as the **Plantations**, the Crown seized rebel estates to give to loyal settlers in order to pacify Irish lands. In 1584 Queen Elizabeth seized 500,000 acres of land on which to settle English Protestant immigrants. When leading Catholic earls rebelled and then fled to the continent in 1607 to seek Spanish help, King James I seized their land and moved thousands of Scottish Presbyterians to 2 million acres in Northern Ireland, displacing many of the native Irish Catholics.

> **Plantations** were the settlement of loyal English and Scottish Protestants in Ireland by the English Crown in the sixteenth and seventeenth centuries, displacing native Catholics from their land.

Irish Catholic anger exploded in 1641, when they took advantage of the civil war then raging in England to rise up and massacre thousands of Protestants, but eventually they were brutally suppressed by Oliver Cromwell in 1649. Cromwell led the parliamentary forces that defeated and executed King Charles I of England, and he shortly became Lord Protector of England. While commanding the forces in Ireland, he executed thousands of rebels and priests and drove 30,000 Catholics to flee to the continent.

In the Act of Settlement of 1652, most of the remaining Catholic land was confiscated from the original Irish landowners. The Irish had one last opportunity to restore their rights when the Catholic James II came to the throne of England in 1685 (he succeeded Charles II, whom Parliament had restored to the throne in 1661), but the English Parliament proved quickly that it would not tolerate a Catholic king who believed in absolutism. They invited the Protestants William of Orange and Mary to take the throne of England. James fled to Ireland, but William followed, broke the Catholic siege of Derry/Londonderry in 1689 and then defeated James's forces at the **Battle of the Boyne** in July 1690—both victories still celebrated by Ulster Unionists in marches each summer. The issues involved in England's "Glorious Revolution" are complex, including the fact that the pope supported William of Orange in the hopes that he would bring English power into an alliance against Louis XIV of France. But the consequences for Ireland were dramatic. England was firmly in control of the island and the old Catholic nobility had been dispossessed.

By 1700 only 7 percent of the land remained in Catholic hands, mostly in the more barren western counties. The 1701 Act of Settlement held that henceforth the British monarch must be Protestant.

> The victory of the Protestant King William at the **Battle of the Boyne** in 1690 is still celebrated with annual parades and bonfires by Protestant groups in Northern Ireland such as the Orange Order.

The Protestant Ascendency

English success in the Glorious Revolution initiated a century of Protestant ascendancy. Catholics were seen as disloyal, and along with loss of property were subject by the monarchy to the restrictions of the **Penal Laws** that built legal barriers between the political, cultural, and economic lives of the Protestant and Catholic communities. Under these laws, no Catholic could vote, hold office, practice law, or hold a lease on land for longer than thirty-one years. Unique restrictions were imposed, such as the one barring any Catholic from owning a horse worth more than five pounds. More important, Irish Catholic religious practices were driven underground, and no schools were allowed that taught the Gaelic (Irish) language or the Catholic catechism. Priests had to register with the government or be branded with a "P" on their cheek. While the imposition of the Penal Laws in practice may not have been as harsh as they read in law, they still clearly established a subordinate legal, political, and economic position for the Irish Catholics, the majority of whom were increasingly poor rural laborers.[4]

> **The Penal Laws** were intended to restrict Irish Catholic economic, political, and cultural activity and thus force them to accept the authority of the British Crown and the Protestant Church of Ireland.

The Scottish Presbyterians who had settled in Ireland during the Plantations and fought alongside

William against James II in 1689 and 1690 were also looked upon with suspicion by the British government. These "dissenters" (from the Church of England) were also forbidden to vote or hold office for much of the 1700s, although they retained their property and, by and large, a more prosperous economic position. Some of them migrated to the American colonies in hopes of finding greater religious and political freedom. But the Presbyterians who remained in Ireland found themselves, in spite of their subordinate civil position, allied with the Anglican elite in their mistrust of the Catholic Pope and in their memories of battles with Irish Catholics in the 1640s and 1680s. As the Catholic community was beginning to form a cultural nationalism rooted in the experience of oppression and rebellion, the more urban Protestant community developed a **siege mentality**. They feared for their minority position within what they saw as a hostile and backward rural Catholic majority and were determined to help the government keep the Catholics in a subordinate position. The triumph of William and Mary and the Act of Settlement guaranteeing a Protestant monarch were hailed as necessary protections for their Protestant culture.

A siege mentality is a defensive attitude caused by fear that one is surrounded by enemies, in this case the determination by Protestants to defend their dominant position by any means necessary lest they lose their rights if Ireland were governed by a Catholic monarch or a majority Catholic Republican population.

Even as a deeper cultural gulf was being established between the two competing national communities, a broader concept of civic nationalism drew the support of some of the educated elite. Civic (or political) nationalists drew on the writings of the Enlightenment and the examples of the American and French Revolutions in the later part of the eighteenth century. Wolfe Tone, a Protestant lawyer in Dublin, was their most famous leader and was one of the founders in 1791 of the Society of United Irishmen.

Using language from the French Declaration of the Rights of Man and Citizen, the United Irishmen argued that the Irish formed one nation in which all men should be treated equally regardless of their religion, and that as a united nation they had the right to rule themselves. Tone argued that if the Catholics seemed ignorant and inferior it was the fault of the British government that had outlawed their schools. "We plunge them by law, and continue them by statute, in gross ignorance, and then we make the incapacity we have created an argument for their exclusion from the common rights of man! We plead our crime in justification of itself. . . . Give them education, open their eyes, shew them what is law. . . . let them be citizens, let them be *men*."[5] He clearly identified Great Britain as the source of Ireland's social and economic ills.

The growth of revolutionary fervor prompted some reforms from the British government, such as permitting Catholic landowners to vote in 1793 (although that affected only a small number since Catholics were still in the minority of landowners) and allowing the establishment of a Catholic seminary to train priests in 1795. Many Irish Protestants, however, were concerned about Tone's concept of Irish nationalism based on a liberal constitution and equal citizenship rights, believing not only that the native Irish were an inferior people who could not understand a democracy based on individual rights but also that equal civil and voting rights would trap Protestants in a state with a Catholic majority. In 1795 they formed the **Orange Order** (harking back to William of Orange) to defend the Protestant ascendancy. The Orange Order and similar groups such as the Apprentice Boys in Derry created rituals and marches that commemorated Protestant victories and demonstrated the superior position of the Loyalists, who were prepared to defend the political ties to England and to protect the Protestant ascendancy.

The Orange Order was a Protestant, Unionist society first formed in 1795 to defend the Protestant ascendancy against rising demands for political rights for Catholics. It is known for its marches to celebrate significant Protestant battles, particularly each 12 July to celebrate King William's victories in 1690.

In 1798 Tone and the United Irishmen attempted to create a general rebellion coordinated with the landing of a small French army, but they failed miserably. Uprisings in Wexford and Ulster were crushed by the British in May and June before the French army even arrived in Mayo in the west in August. The British under Gen. Charles Cornwallis defeated the French in September. (Cornwallis is remembered by Americans for surrendering to them at the Battle of Yorktown in 1781. He served as lord lieutenant of Ireland from 1798 to 1801.) Thousands of rebels were hung, others were flogged or transported to British colonies. Wolfe Tone himself was captured in November and committed suicide in prison rather than face execution. To better control Ireland, Britain (as it faced continuing warfare with Napoleonic France) decided to abolish the Irish parliament and exercise direct rule over the island. Parliament passed the **Act of Union** in 1800, establishing the United Kingdom of Great Britain and Ireland. The Act of Union cemented Protestant domination, but the failure of the United Irishmen provided martyrs to drive the dreams of Irish Republicanism.

The **Act of Union.** After the failed rebellion of the United Irishmen in 1798, the British government determined to exercise direct rule over Ireland by abolishing the Irish parliament and giving the Irish seats in the British Houses of Parliament at Westminster, establishing the United Kingdom of Great Britain and Ireland on 1 January 1801.

The Growth of Cultural Nationalisms in the Nineteenth and Twentieth Centuries

In the 1800s, Irish Nationalists divided between those who advocated violence and those who sought peaceful reform through mass rallies and elections. Early in the century, Catholic farmers frustrated with the legal system that favored Protestant landlords formed rural secret societies like the "White Boys" to defend Catholic peasants against practices such as rack-renting (raising rents to drive Catholic peasants off the land) through small-scale violence. Most Catholics were tenant farmers who cultivated fewer than fifteen acres or were landless workers. The cultivation of the potato (which provided more calories per acre than any other available crop) allowed the population to grow to over 8 million by 1840, but that growth put severe pressure on limited resources. While Protestant towns in the North developed industry, and Anglican landlords raised cattle and grain to export to England, the reliance of the land-starved Catholic poor on one crop proved disastrous. Disease hit the potato crop in the Great Famine from 1845 to 1848, and the lack of food combined with government mismanagement of the crisis led to the deaths through starvation and disease of up to 1.5 million people and the emigration of 1 million more.

The vulnerability caused by reliance on a single crop was worsened by the laissez-faire ideology of the Whig government in Britain. Reluctant to interfere in the laws of free trade by buying more grain on the world market to feed the starving, it continued to export grain from Ireland to England while woefully underfunding work schemes for the poor. Those policies were in large part driven by an elite prejudice that blamed the overpopulation and poverty on the moral failings of the Irish themselves. The *Times* stated in March 1847, "We have to change the very nature of a people born and bred from time immemorial in inveterate indolence, improvidence, disobedience, and consequently destitution."[6] Many officials believed that the famine provided the opportunity to consolidate larger estates by driving off the poor (through deaths or evictions) and thus reform the island's economic system. Indeed, they believed that the famine was a divine judgment on the Irish poor, and thus efforts at aid and relief were tragically insufficient. In turn, Irish Nationalists blamed the suffering on deliberate British policies of extermination. The famine remained a powerful symbol of British oppression into the twentieth century.

The poverty of the rural classes endured and led to a continued out-migration that finally totaled 6 million Irish men and women across the nineteenth century, leaving the Irish population in 1900 at half what it had been in 1840. Hatred of Britain for the deaths in the famine and for the repression of a small desperate revolt in 1848 by a group called Young Ireland led to the emergence in 1858 of an organization that continued the tradition of armed resistance to British rule and Protestant landlords. Labeled the **"Fenians,"** the most ardent Republicans formed the underground **Irish Republican Brotherhood** (IRB) and kept alive the hope of defeating the British through force in order to establish an independent Irish Republican state. Although retaining part of Tone's rhetoric about the need for a secular state that established individual freedoms, they also played upon Catholic discontents that were not only political but also economic. Their attempt at a rebellion in 1867 was easily suppressed, but—along with pressure from the Irish National Land League that led protests and boycotts against landowners in the 1870s and 1880s—it did prompt Britain into modest reforms.

Fenians were members of a secret underground Irish Nationalist society (also active in the United States and Britain) that failed in an attempt to overthrow British rule in Ireland in 1867. The society lived on through the **Irish Republican Brotherhood**. The name derives from the Fianna Éireann, a legendary band of ancient Irish warriors. Protestants frequently used the word as a derogatory term for any Irish Catholic.

Each failed uprising or protest at least kept alive the Republican cultural tradition. These actions also hardened the attitudes of the Protestant community and the Loyalists' fears of the Catholic rebels. Unionist politicians allied to the Conservative Party in the British Parliament frequently played the "Orange card," an overt appeal to Protestant prejudices and fears, while periodically inciting riots against local Catholic neighborhoods in the North. Playing on sectarian (religious) fears, they could win elections in counties with Protestant majorities and reaffirm the suppression of the Catholic community by the state. Just as a more aggressive Republican culture developed among Nationalists, an equally aggressive defensive culture developed among many Unionists.[7]

Other Nationalist groups rejected violence and attempted to use lawful means and mass politics to bring about reforms. Prior to the famine, Daniel O'Connell led the political campaigns that resulted in Parliament's grant of Catholic emancipation in 1829. Emancipation allowed Catholics to sit in Parliament, hold government offices, and practice legal professions, although the vote was still restricted to landowners, so Catholics remained a minority of voters. But with further midcentury reforms the Catholic vote grew, while being joined by some Protestants who also longed for Ireland to assume greater control of its destiny rather than be ruled directly from London.

The dominant issue by the 1880s was the Nationalists' quest for **Irish Home Rule**, a restoration of the Irish parliament while remaining within the United Kingdom. The Irish Parliamentary Party, composed of both Protestant and Catholic members of Parliament (MPs) was led by the Anglo-Irish Protestant landlord Charles Stuart Parnell. It took advantage of national agitation over land reform and mass political strategies to win eighty-six seats in the British Parliament by 1886. When Parliament was closely divided between the mainstream Conservative and Liberal (and later Labour) Parties, the Irish Parliamentary Party might determine the majority and thus could try to use its leverage to get Parliament to reestablish an Irish parliament (devolution). They hoped Ireland would be able to exercise authority over local government similarly to the dominion status established for Canada (1867) and Australia (1901). Conservatives in the British Parliament blocked attempts to pass Irish

Home Rule bills in 1886 and 1892. When the issue returned in 1912, the British found that the delay in reform had allowed opinions to radicalize on both sides and the two clearly opposed concepts of Irish national identity to harden.

"Irish Home Rule" was the term used to describe the attempt to return local autonomy and government to Ireland within the larger United Kingdom before World War I. It is also referred to as devolution.

The Home Rule Crisis and Rebellion

By 1900, Ireland was dealing with four distinct unresolved issues. The first was equal civil status: the British had advanced reforms in political status through granting Catholic Emancipation and voting rights that brought more equal civil and political rights including liberty of religious expression, but the reforms had resulted in little real political power for the Catholic community. The second problem was economic disparity: unequal land distribution and limited Catholic ownership was still pressing. In 1901, Britain finally passed a Land Purchase Act that helped some 300,000 tenants buy their land by World War I, but the greater economic disparity remained. The third issue was cultural authenticity: while Unionists held tight to their British and Protestant identities, Nationalists realized that to justify their own separate sovereign state the Irish had to clearly establish an Irish national identity that was separate from Britain. Fourth was the question of national autonomy: creating cultural institutions that reflected the Catholic majority led to increasing calls for national independence. Both civic and cultural nationalists saw Ireland's economic problems as part of the political problem of British "colonial" rule. Parliament's unwillingness to grant Home Rule seemed to confirm for Nationalists that only independence from Britain could allow the Irish people to rule themselves and achieve their potential. Unionists, meanwhile, feared the loss of their rights as British citizens if the connection to the United Kingdom was broken.[8]

By 1901 a mere 0.5 percent of the Irish population spoke the Irish language alone, and only about 14 percent could understand it. Increasingly, both Catholic and a small but influential group of Protestant Nationalists believed that a revival of the Irish language and literature and a recapturing of Irish traditions in areas as wide-ranging as folklore and sport could build a common sense of national identity and justify a collective mobilization against British dominance. For many, the Catholic religion was part of that tradition, but others drew on the ancient legends and medieval history of Ireland to imagine a moral identity that contrasted Irish communitarian and spiritual values against British greed and commercialism.

With constitutional reform seemingly blocked in Parliament, the underground movement to force Britain to leave Ireland through violence grew in strength. Pluralist civic nationalists, who advocated peaceful political action to achieve Home Rule involving all religious faiths in Ireland, seemed increasingly ineffective. The Irish Republican Brotherhood was convinced that the British would never voluntarily give up Ireland and rejected participation in parliamentary elections because participation would seem to recognize the legitimacy of British rule. The IRB planned ultimately to use violence to drive the British out and organized in small cells so that secrecy could be maintained. It received support from Irish émigrés in the United States in an organization named Clan na Gael that raised money and arms for the cause.

Many Irish intellectuals believed that for the political movement to succeed the Irish needed to develop a stronger sense of national identity separate from English culture. These educators and writers who led the study of ancient Gaelic folklore and revived Irish literature and poetry came from mixed backgrounds, both Protestant and Catholic. William Butler Yeats and Augusta Lady Gregory, for example, were Anglo-Irish Protestants who formed the Abbey Theatre in Dublin in 1904 and promoted theater and literature that explored Irish themes and culture even though written in English. But in the same decades, cultural nationalists such as D. P. Moran rejected a broader civic and political nationalism that included all the religions that existed in Ireland and criticized as elitist the development of a literary culture open only to the intelligentsia. Moran instead insisted that Ireland should be self-governing and that it should develop its own manners, customs, literature, and economic independence (expressed in "Buy Irish" campaigns and movements to open Protestant professions to Catholics) rooted in a moral code drawn not just from the ancient history and traditional heroes of Ireland but also from the common historical experience of defending their nation and their religion. For him Catholicism was the cultural force that bound the nation together.[9]

TIP Read Sections B and C of the core texts to further explore the competing concepts of nationalism in Northern Ireland.

Earlier in the 1880s, Catholic archbishop Thomas Croke (a promoter of the Irish National Land League) had already condemned English literature, theater, and sports as promoting immorality. By the 1890s and early 1900s, a large number of organizations, uncoordinated and sometimes at odds on methods, pushed for the development of a native Irish culture separate from the British. The Gaelic League, formed in 1893 to stop the erosion of the Irish language, had 600 branches by 1904. Cultural leaders such as Eoin McNeill and Patrick Pearse founded Irish-language newspapers and schools, leading in 1908 to the establishment of the National University, which required the study of Irish by all its students. Nationalists revived Irish games such as Gaelic football and hurling to distinguish themselves from sports developed in English public schools such as football (soccer) and rugby.

As opposed to the United Irishmen's pluralistic civic view of national identity, Irish nationalists by the early 1900s increasingly advocated a more narrowly ethnic and linguistic cultural nationalism. A new political party founded in 1906, **Sinn Féin** (translated literally, "We Ourselves"), led by Arthur Griffith, embodied the movement to reject Home Rule within the United Kingdom and insist on a complete separation from Britain. Sinn Féin advocated self-sufficiency to protect the Irish nation from an economic dependency on Britain, rejected service in the British military, and argued for nonrecognition of the authority of the Parliament in Westminster. It urged Irish MPs to abstain from service in Parliament and instead advocated establishing a separate Irish parliament with its own civil service and courts.[10]

Sinn Féin was established in 1906 as a nationalist party that advocated creating an Irish Republic independent of the United Kingdom.

The growth of an Irish Catholic Nationalism caused increasing concerns among Protestant Unionists who were loyal to the United Kingdom. Unionists were concerned that Home Rule would lead to a Catholic majority in any Irish legislature and thus endanger their economic dominance and their religious interests. The Protestants saw themselves as superior culturally to the native Irish peoples and were convinced that the industrial and urban prosperity of Ulster would be threatened by domination by rural Ireland. They feared **"Rome Rule,"** which would subject their religious liberties to Catholic moral law, such as the insistence on priestly celibacy and that the children of mixed marriages must be raised Catholic, and they could point to the papacy's condemnation of liberal democracy in the nineteenth century. Frequently, Unionist MPs at Westminster provided the votes necessary to block political reform. Just as Nationalist extremists believed that only force could induce Britain to withdraw from Ireland, Unionist extremists increasingly threatened their own use of violence to retain British Protestant control of the island.[11]

Rome Rule was shorthand for Protestant fears of becoming a minority population within a united Ireland dominated by the Catholic Church and its pope in Rome.

The British Liberal Party had the opportunity in 1911 to strip the conservative House of Lords of its power to block reform bills passed by the House of Commons. John Redmond, then head of the Irish Party in Parliament, offered the support of his MPs to the Liberals in return for submission of a new Home Rule bill for Ireland in 1912. Ulster Unionists led by Edward Carson and John Craig immediately reacted against this threat of being placed under a Catholic-dominated Home Rule government in Dublin. They were aided by British Conservatives who played the "Orange card" and supported Protestant resistance to any form of Home Rule. The leader of the British Conservative Party, Andrew Bonar Law, in a speech in 1912 stated that the Irish Unionists would be justified in resisting the government plans for Home Rule by all means in their possession, including force. One hundred thousand Unionists marched in military formation in Belfast to indicate their opposition, and by September 1912, 500,000 Protestants had signed the Ulster Covenant pledging to refuse to recognize the authority of Parliament and to "stand by one another in defending, for ourselves and our children, our cherished position of equal citizenship in the United Kingdom, and in using all means which may be found necessary to defeat the present conspiracy to set up a Home Rule Parliament in Ireland" (see core text no. 6). By 1913, the Unionists had enrolled 150,000 volunteers in a paramilitary organization, the **Ulster Volunteer Force (UVF)**, which began to smuggle weapons into the country.[12]

Through enrolling recruits in the **Ulster Volunteer Force (UVF),** Protestant Unionists threatened Britain with civil war in 1912–13 if Parliament approved a Home Rule government for a United Ireland.

Irish Nationalists responded by creating their own paramilitary force, the Irish Volunteers led by Eoin MacNeill. If Britain would not protect Catholics, they vowed they would defend themselves. "They have rights who dare to maintain them," MacNeill proclaimed.[13] Many of their leaders were also members of the secret Irish Republican Brotherhood. Ireland seemed on the verge of civil war over Home Rule, a crisis made worse by massive labor strikes. Attacked by the police in the Lockout of 1913, the striking workers led by James Connolly began to organize a third force, the Citizen Army. Meanwhile, British army officers made it clear they would refuse to use their troops against the Unionist paramilitary organization, the Ulster Volunteers. The British Cabinet was only saved from a severe crisis in Ireland by the outbreak of World War I in August 1914, which it used as an excuse to suspend the implementation of Home Rule until after the war. But it quietly gave assurances to the Loyalists in the northern counties of Ireland that they would be granted a separate devolved government and would not be forced to join the lower twenty-six counties where the Catholics held a majority.

Irish Nationalists split over their reaction to World War I. The parliamentary party led by Redmond urged Catholics to join Protestants in volunteering to serve in the British army against Germany. Over 200,000 Irish men of all faiths volunteered; an estimated 35,000 died. Redmond hoped that service in the war would prove the loyalty of Ireland to the Crown and lead to the introduction of Home Rule as soon as the war ended. But Sinn Féin refused to cooperate with the war effort. For that party and for leaders of the Irish Republican Brotherhood, Home Rule was not sufficient. They yearned for a Republic that gave the Irish people their own sovereign state free of any tie to the United Kingdom—the ultimate fulfillment of the cultural nationalism that had developed by 1914.

With Britain distracted by the continuing costly war in Europe, the leaders of the IRB saw an opportunity to strike. By instigating a rebellion to establish an Irish Republic, they hoped either to cause a mass uprising that would end British rule in Ireland, or, if defeated, to provide new martyrs for the cause of Irish independence, revive nationalist fervor, and get the issue of an independent Ireland onto the table of the peace talks that would take place at the end of the war. Led by Patrick Pearse, Tom Clarke, Sean Mac-

Dermott, Joseph Plunkett, and Thomas MacDonagh and joined by union leader James Connolly, they originally planned to start an insurrection of the Irish Volunteers on Easter Sunday 1916. When MacNeill learned that an attempt to smuggle in arms from Germany for the IRB had failed, he cancelled the call for the Volunteers to carry out maneuvers across the country on Easter since he believed that without the weapons they could not succeed. But the leaders in Dublin determined to go forward with an uprising in the city itself the next day. Pearse had previously claimed that "bloodshed is a cleansing and a sanctifying thing, and the nation which regards it as the final horror has lost its manhood" (see core text no. 10). He cited the model of the Irish legendary hero Cuchulainn: "I care not if I live but one day and one night, if my fame and deeds live after me," and connected the deaths that would come in a violent uprising to the blood sacrifice of Jesus Christ.[14] Even if the rebellion failed, its leaders believed that out of their sacrifice would spring a living nation. The IRB, now the Irish Republican Army (IRA), was supported by a Republican women's organization, the Cumann na mBan, and was joined by Connolly's Citizen Army, who hoped a revolution for a Republic would also produce the first step toward a socialist state.

Thus, although they knew that the uprising in the countryside had been thwarted, the IRA rose on Easter Monday, 24 April 1916, and seized control of key buildings in Dublin, most famously the General Post Office (GPO), the center of communication and symbol of empire on O'Connell Street. Pearse stood in front of the GPO and read out "The Proclamation of the Provisional Government of the Irish Republic," citing the obligation of the generation of 1916 to past generations of revolutionaries, using previous rebellions to claim legitimacy for the present fight for independence.

> We declare the right of the people of Ireland to the ownership of Ireland and to the unfettered control of Irish destinies, to be sovereign and indefeasible. The long usurpation of that right by a foreign people has not extinguished the right. . . . In every generation the Irish people have asserted their right to national freedom and sovereignty. . . . Standing on that fundamental right and again asserting it by arms in the face of the world, we hereby proclaim the Irish Republic as a Sovereign Independent State, and we pledge our lives and the lives of our comrades-in-arms to the cause of its freedom. (Core text no. 11.)

Although taken by surprise, the British government reacted quickly, cutting the rebels off from the rest of the country and bringing in reinforcements by railroad. By the middle of the week the British army began to use weapons of modern war—artillery and machine guns—to destroy the rebel strongholds as well as much of the city center. By Saturday, the rebels surrendered.

Initially, popular opinion stood against the rebels and blamed them for a hopeless battle that devastated Dublin. But British mishandling of the aftermath soon turned many Irish against the United Kingdom. Gen. John Maxwell, commander of the British forces, declared martial law, arresting some 3,500 people. In early May he ordered the secret court-martials and rapid executions of fifteen of the leaders, including Pearse, Clarke, MacDermott, Plunkett, MacDonagh, and Connolly. Public hostility grew against the British government for depriving the defendants of a fair trial and for using excessive force in destroying parts of Dublin. Popular support for Republicanism increased in 1918, when the British attempted to introduce conscription in Ireland to help replace its losses of soldiers on the Western Front.

The rebellion and its aftermath cemented the conflict between the two competing cultural communities. *For Unionists, the **Easter Rising** was a treasonous attempt at a violent coup by an unelected group of terrorists.* Protestants condemned the rebels and the Irish Republican Army for stabbing Britain in the back at the very moment it was fighting to save democracy in the trenches in France. It was proof that Catholics were disloyal and led the Unionists to demand a separate six-county state in Ulster. (In fact,

Unionists for the next century would point to the sacrifices they made for Great Britain in the war against Germany in contrast to the Republican rebellion; particularly in July 1916, when 2,000 men of the Thirty-Sixth Ulster division were killed and 3,000 wounded at the Battle of the Somme. Most of these soldiers were volunteers who had been members of the Ulster Volunteer Force.)

The Easter Rising of 1916, while a failure militarily for the Irish Republican Army, spurred the growth of Sinn Féin, who cited it as the origin of the Irish Republic.

For Nationalists, the declaration of martial law and harsh justice by the British breathed new inspiration into Republicanism. Pearse and the other leaders were praised for their courage and self-sacrifice in poems, stories, plays, posters, and souvenirs. Their martyrdom was frequently depicted using a blend of Catholic and Irish Nationalist imagery, as in William Butler Yeats's poem "The Rose Tree" (1921), in which he had Pearse and Connolly discussing how to revise the Irish nation (the rose tree) and concluding, "There's nothing but our own red blood, can make a right Rose Tree." Such language made the Rising a mythic event where the rebels redeemed the shame of Ireland's past failures and proclaimed an independent, sovereign Republic. It showed that the spirit of the Irish nation with its soul of honor and bravery could not be crushed by British power with its material greed and violent militarism.

Redmond and the parliamentary party that had advocated a broader civic nationalism looking for peaceful reform within the United Kingdom rapidly lost the support of voters. Sinn Féin, although it had not participated as a party in the uprising, benefited as the party clearly advocating a complete break with the United Kingdom. Eamon de Valera (a prominent member of Sinn Féin who had also been a commander in the IRB during the rebellion and only escaped execution in 1916 because he was a US citizen) led the building of hundreds of Sinn Féin branches across the country. Meanwhile **Michael Collins** directed the military arm of the movement, building the IRB/IRA into an organization capable of fighting the first modern guerrilla war against an imperial power. Prominent Catholic clergy, who had condemned the lawlessness of the Fenians in the nineteenth century, now clearly identified with the goals of the Nationalists. Priests presided over the funerals of republicans and declared that the Irish had the right to resist conscription into the British army "by every means that are consonant with the laws of God."[15] When the first election for the British Parliament after the end of World War I took place in December 1918, Sinn Féin swept to victory, winning seventy-three of the seats allocated to Ireland versus twenty-six seats for Unionist candidates and only six for the moderate Irish Party. It proved to be the last all-Ireland election.

Michael Collins and the IRA provided a blueprint for colonial independence movements by using assassinations and guerrilla tactics to force the British Empire to the negotiating table.

Rather than take their seats in the British Parliament at Westminster, the Sinn Féin MPs determined that as the representatives of the Irish people they had the right to set up their own independent government. They met in Dublin in January 1919 and constituted themselves as the Irish National Assembly, the Dáil Éireann. They issued a declaration of independence, stating that "the Irish Republic was proclaimed in Dublin on Easter Monday, 1916, by the Irish Republican Army, acting on behalf of the Irish people." They demanded that the British evacuate Ireland and began setting up their own administration.

Instead of leaving, the British declared the Dáil, Sinn Féin, and the IRB/IRA illegal and struck back with force in the Anglo-Irish War of 1919–22. The IRA used tactics of ambush and assassination to try to make the British decide that the war was not worth the human and economic cost. On "Bloody Sunday" in November 1920, for example, Collins's elite "Squad" assassinated twelve British secret intelligence officers. When arrested as a member of the IRA, the mayor of Cork, Terence MacSwiney, refused to recognize the authority of the court that tried him and died after a seventy-three-day hunger strike. He was lauded as a martyr who demonstrated the devotion of Republicans to their cause. The British struck back hard, recruiting and organizing World War I veterans into military units known as the Black and Tans, which carried out brutal reprisals against villages and towns that harbored rebels. In response to Bloody Sunday, for example, a Black and Tans unit drove armored cars into the middle of an All-Ireland Final Gaelic Football match at Croke Park and indiscriminately fired into the crowd, killing eleven and wounding dozens more. These tactics only turned the population more strongly against the British presence.

The British attempted to solve the problem by drafting a new Home Rule bill that split Ireland into the six counties of the North, with a majority Protestant population, and the twenty-six counties of the South, with a majority Catholic population. While Sinn Féin continued to reject any cooperation with Britain, the Unionists in Northern Ireland eagerly began creating their own separate government. In Northern Ireland a new assembly was elected in 1921, with the loyalist Ulster Unionist Party winning forty out of fifty-two seats.

In December 1921, the British and Sinn Féin, in mutual exhaustion, accepted a ceasefire and began negotiations. But even then, the British were not ready to grant a republic or to abandon the Unionists in Northern Ireland who had been loyal to the United Kingdom. The British insisted on maintaining the **partition of Ireland**. Northern Ireland would keep its own devolved government within the United Kingdom. The South would be given dominion status as the Irish Free State but still remain within the British Commonwealth—members of the Dáil would be required to take an oath of loyalty to the British monarch, and the British navy retained access to key ports.

Northern Ireland was officially **partitioned** by Britain and elected its first assembly in 1921; an arrangement ratified in 1922 in the treaty between Britain and the Irish Dáil that led to the establishment of the Irish Free State in the southern counties, ending the Anglo-Irish War.

The chief Irish negotiators, Michael Collins and Arthur Griffith, accepted the treaty as the best they could get. Collins recognized that the IRA did not have the resources to continue the war indefinitely but believed that accepting the Free State could be the first step toward an independent Irish Republic. Eamon de Valera bitterly opposed the agreement because of its continuing link to the British Crown, but it was approved by the Dáil in June 1922 on a sixty-four to fifty-seven vote and then ratified by a plebiscite among the Irish people. De Valera and Republican hardliners rejected the outcome of the vote, split Sinn Féin in two, and led a civil war against the new Irish Free State. Their forces were defeated in 1923 and the Irish Free State was confirmed as the government of the twenty-six counties in the south of Ireland.

THE DEVELOPMENT OF TWO IRELANDS

Solidifying Two Separate National Communities: Southern and Northern Ireland after 1922

During the twentieth century, the Unionists used the authority devolved from the British Parliament to set up a government in Northern Ireland; while the Irish Free State evolved in the South, slowly establishing more independence from the British Empire until it proclaimed itself the Republic of Ireland in 1948. Both governments were secular states with individual rights established, such as freedom of religion. But each used its own cultural nationalism to build unique identities around institutions that protected the positions of the Protestant community in the North and advanced the Catholic moral identity and the Irish language and culture in the South. The strong cultural and ethnic identity of each community allowed each in turn to maintain traditional fears and stereotypes. While we will concentrate more on the developing conditions in Northern Ireland, it is important to note important aspects of the developments in the South that helped maintain a strong barrier between the competing national communities.

From the Irish Free State to the Republic of Ireland: Building a Unique Identity in the Rural Catholic South

The treaty that established the Irish Free State was at best a compromise, one that Michael Collins and his supporters hoped would eventually lead to unification of Ireland. But the bitter civil war that resulted in the assassination of Collins by Irish Republicans and the deaths of 4,000 to 5,000 people overall led the Free State to use military and counterterrorist methods to subdue antitreaty Republican forces led by de Valera. Those forces ended the fighting in the spring of 1923, looking for another way to advance their political cause.

The Irish Free State established a democracy through a written constitution that called for the election of a 153-seat Dáil through proportional representation and guaranteed the protection of the rights of minorities. It formed an unarmed civil guard to establish adequate policing and win back the trust of the people, who were tired of the violence of the civil war. By and large the state was conservative economically and dependent on agriculture. Political parties emerged, split between those who had supported the treaty (Cumann na Gaedheal) that later developed into Fine Gael, and those from the old Sinn Féin who saw the Free State as a British puppet and who initially abstained from sitting in the Dáil. But in 1926 **Eamon de Valera** decided to end abstentionism and set up a new party, Fianna Fáil, to contest elections and win control of the government through elections. By 1932 Fianna Fáil won a plurality of votes in the Dáil and de Valera, who had the heroic aura of being the last commander left alive from the rebellion of 1916, became prime minister (taoiseach [TAY-shuh]) for the first time. He held that position until 1959, with only two three-year absences, and then became president of Ireland until 1973.

Eamon de Valera, elected as prime minister, or president, of Ireland for forty years, helped to establish its rural, Catholic, and Irish identity, neutral in world affairs.

De Valera and Fianna Fáil were committed to restoring the unity of Ireland and to making Ireland self-sufficient by establishing as many families as possible on the land. In a new constitution of 1937, they included clauses that made clear Ireland's claim to the six counties lost to Northern Ireland. They accelerated a revolutionary policy started in the 1920s to revive Irish culture. The teaching of the Irish language was made compulsory in the schools—and, in the primary schools particularly, more concrete subjects such as science lost space to teaching the Irish language and culture. About one-third of the schools held instruction only in Irish, whereas most of the rest mixed Irish and English. Catholic moral teaching infused the social and educational legislation of the Free State. The Catholic hierarchy was not directly involved in ruling, but its influence seemed obvious to Protestant loyalists. Irish laws forbade divorce and contraception, and a censorship board blocked the publication of material that was found objectionable to morals. Mothers were discouraged from working in order to protect the traditional concept of the family. Fear of the direction of the new state had already led up to a third of the Protestants who lived in the twenty-six southern counties to leave the Irish Free State by 1926.

The IRA and other paramilitary organizations were outlawed in 1931 as the Free State determined to demilitarize the population and establish a professional army. But de Valera demonstrated his continuing hostility to Great Britain in other ways—setting up high tariffs to try to reduce Irish economic dependence on British trade and expanding the land under tillage in an attempt to make Ireland self-sufficient. The Irish government ended the requirement that members of the Dáil swear an oath of allegiance to the British monarch in 1933. In the new constitution of 1937, the Free State was renamed Eire. In 1948, its government finally broke with the British Commonwealth and officially adopted the title of the Republic of Ireland. Not only did the constitution continue to lay claim to Northern Ireland but in Article 44 it made clear its cultural and ethnic character: "The state recognizes the special position of the Holy Catholic Apostolic Church and Roman Church" (see core text no. 12). Unionists looking on from Northern Ireland were appalled by the influence of the Catholic Church, and they were offended when de Valera kept Eire neutral during World War II. In Unionist eyes he had stabbed Britain in the back by the rebellion of 1916 and now he refused to help protect democracy from the Nazi threat.

The Republic's emphasis on agriculture and its resistance to industrialization and urbanization held back its economic development. It also did not enact the kind of social welfare reforms and national health services established by Britain and most of the rest of Western Europe after 1945. The lack of development meant that citizens of the Irish state had a lower standard of living than the British until the 1990s. Perhaps most indicative of that economic stagnation was the continued emigration of hundreds of thousands of Irish to foreign countries until the population had fallen to just less than 3 million by 1961. Added to Protestant religious and political grievances against the Republic of Ireland, the contrast in economic development into the 1960s helped underline Unionist determination to remain part of the United Kingdom and to cling to the rights they had as British citizens. Still, the Republic of Ireland succeeded in developing its own clearly unique identity that lent inspiration to Catholic Nationalists who were trapped as a minority in Northern Ireland by the events of 1921–23.

The Republic of Ireland did develop new economic policies in the 1960s and 1970s that encouraged outside investment and the development of tourism. By 1971 there were more urban than rural workers for the first time. At the same time the spread of television and an easing of censorship allowed the development of a more modern culture that could begin to challenge some of the restrictions of the Church. The Church itself began to change some of its traditional practices and engage in open dialogue with other religious traditions after the Vatican II Council (1962–65). Free public secondary education was established in 1967, and modern subjects and science replaced mandatory instruction in Irish. The population began to grow again. The Republic joined the European Community in 1973, dropping trade barriers and leading Ireland to become the home for a number of firms, particularly in technology, that did business with Europe. By the 1990s, the standard of living was rising toward the level in Britain. But in spite of the modernization of the South, Northern Unionists still believed they had clear differences with the Irish Nationalist community and still feared Ireland's ultimate claim over the six counties in Northern Ireland. The clearly Republican and Catholic identity of Ireland from the 1920s to the 1960s helped the Unionists to rationalize their construction of a community based on the protection of Protestant and British civilization in Northern Ireland.

Northern Ireland: Establishing a One-Party Protestant State That Controls a Catholic Minority

The Ulster Unionist Party, initially led by James Craig as the first prime minister of Northern Ireland, dominated Ulster for the next fifty years after winning the initial election in 1921. Craig's goal was to build a Protestant state for a Protestant people with defensible borders against the imminent Nationalist threat of the Irish Free State. In 1926, two-thirds of the total population of 1,250,000 were Protestant (Presbyterians and Anglicans) and one-third were Catholic. The UUP believed in endurance, self-reliance, and faith as Protestant values versus what they saw as the backward culture of the superstitious and treacherous Catholics. They feared that any Catholic would be disloyal to Northern Ireland and to Britain and probably was a secret member of the IRA. One UUP leader stated in 1934, "I recommend those who are Loyalists not to employ Roman Catholics, 99 percent of whom are probably disloyal."[16] They believed they had to defend themselves from the Catholic majority in the rest of Ireland and invoked the siege mentality that had existed since the siege of Derry/Londonderry in 1689. The Unionists insisted on their loyalty to the United Kingdom and cited their sacrifices to save democracy and British values in World War I and World War II in contrast to the treachery of the Republicans in 1916 and the neutrality of Ireland in the 1940s. Unionists saw politics as a zero-sum game of victory or defeat against the Nationalists and were suspicious of any move that Britain made that might weaken its protection of Ulster.

Determined to protect the new government in Stormont (the common name given to the Parliament buildings in Northern Ireland, located in the Stormont Estate area in Belfast), the Northern Irish government created a police force, the **Royal Ulster Constabulary**, that was overwhelmingly Protestant and recruited auxiliary policemen, the **"B Specials"** from the ranks of the Loyalist Ulster Volunteer Force. These police stood by or even participated in mob action that drove 5,000 Catholic workers from their jobs in the Belfast shipyards in 1920 and 1921 and burned thousands of Catholics out of their homes.

The **Special Powers Act** of 1922 gave the RUC sweeping powers to maintain order, including trying offenses in special courts without juries, and permitted methods such as flogging and internment (arrest without trial).

The **Royal Ulster Constabulary** and the **B Specials** (auxiliary police later reformed as the Ulster Defence Regiment) were overwhelmingly Protestant and used the tools of the **Special Powers Act** to keep the Nationalist population under control.

While the IRA continued an underground existence, it was weak and only carried out small sporadic campaigns of violence that failed to gain any concessions. The UUP carefully controlled elections, ending proportional representation in the 1920s to base the franchise on property ownership and thus increasing the voting advantage of the majority Protestants. In local areas that had populations with Catholic majorities, such as Derry/Londonderry, the UUP created gerrymandered districts that placed Protestant majorities in town councils. (Gerrymandering is the manipulation of the borders of electoral districts to favor one political party or cultural group.) The Protestant-dominated councils overtly favored Protestants in employment, education, and housing. When Northern Ireland's industries (particularly shipbuilding and linen production) declined after World War II, the Catholics suffered a higher unemployment rate and the province became dependent on Great Britain's social welfare state. The division was clear. Catholics and Protestants by and large lived segregated lives. In polls taken in the early 1960s, 74 percent of Catholics believed they were discriminated against, while an equal number of Protestants believed there was no discrimination.

THE TROUBLES, 1967–1998

The label "the Troubles," first applied to the warfare between Ireland and Britain that lasted from 1916 to 1922, was once again used to describe the decades-long sectarian warfare that roiled Northern Ireland in the last half of the twentieth century. Given the scale of global atrocities, the human cost of the Troubles seems relatively minor: approximately 3,600 dead and 40,000 injured. But Northern Ireland is a small place, with a population of about 1.5 million. The impact of the conflict there becomes more apparent when we regard it proportionally. If this level of ethnic violence had occurred in Britain, it would have resulted in 100,000 dead; in the United States, 500,000. To register the true horror of the Troubles, we need then to imagine a conflict roughly on a par with the American Civil War. The fact that it was drawn out over decades heightened the trauma that afflicted generations of Northern Irish.

A third of these victims were Catholic civilians, another third were security forces (the Royal Ulster Constabulary and its auxiliaries, the British army), the remainder were Protestant civilians (about 20 percent of the total) as well as members of various paramilitary organizations.[17] The Irish Republican Army, the paramilitary associated with the Catholic Nationalist minority, was responsible for a little over half of these deaths. The IRA directed its violence primarily toward the security forces, but its death toll included significant civilian casualties. The Loyalist paramilitaries associated with the Protestant Unionist majority accounted for almost a third of the deaths, largely Catholic civilians targeted for sectarian assassination. Of the remaining victims, the security forces were responsible for slightly over 10 percent (although this figure would be higher if their collusion with the Loyalist paramilitaries were taken into consideration), while the rest died at the hands of unknown perpetrators.[18]

The impact of the violence was intensified by the intimacy of the slaughter. Over 1,000 of those deaths occurred within a mile radius of the interface between the Catholic and Protestant working-class enclaves near Belfast city center. In that claustrophobic space, the tit-for-tat, retributive killings that characterized much of the violence often involved people who were familiar with one another, who at least recognized the faces of their killers or their victims. The criteria for who was attacked were indiscriminately broad. In some cases, it was merely a matter of one's sectarian identity: one member of a Loyalist paramilitary indicated that he had killed a man "for no reason other than he was a Catholic."[19] In other cases, even a tangential and benign association with the security forces put one at risk: the IRA regarded anyone from the grocer who provided fresh vegetables to the RUC (police) headquarters to the garage owner who sold gasoline to a British military vehicle as a "legitimate target."[20]

The 1960s Civil Rights Movement and the Beginning of the Troubles

Why did a society that had existed for almost half a century in a condition of uneasy stasis suddenly explode into sectarian violence?

As noted above, the partitioned state of Northern Ireland was governed by "a Protestant parliament for a Protestant people." This reduced the Catholic minority, a third of the population, to the status of second-class citizens, subjected to discrimination in employment, housing, politics, and law. The unemployment rate for Catholics was twice as high as it was for Protestants, as the Protestant establishment systematically restricted Catholic access to jobs. This attitude percolated downward throughout all levels of Northern Irish society.

The ability of Catholics to redress this situation through political means suffered from the elimination of proportional voting in 1929 in favor of a simple majority rule, a change that significantly diminished the representation of minority political parties in Parliament. At the local level the situation was even worse. Voting for local council elections was restricted to ratepayers and their spouses (that is, those who paid property taxes), a policy that disproportionally disenfranchised Catholic voters. When coupled with extensive gerrymandering, the result was that places like **Derry/Londonderry**, the second-largest city in Northern Ireland, were consistently governed by a Protestant-dominated city council despite having a population whose significant majority was Catholic. Because of this electoral structure, local housing authorities privileged Protestants over Catholics in the allotment of new housing stock in order to restrict the number of Catholic ratepayers and thus voters. Occasionally, as in the case of the Protestant chairman of a housing committee in Enniskillen in County Tyrone, they were overt about their intentions: "We are going to see that the right people are put in these houses, and we are not going to apologise for it."[21] The result was that the Catholic population was sequestered into densely crowded, dilapidated housing in areas such as Derry/Londonderry's Bogside.

Nationalists and Catholics called the same city **Derry**; Unionists and Protestants referred to the city as **Londonderry**. Through gerrymandering, redrawing the electoral districts to favor Unionists, the government made sure that the city council had a Protestant majority even though the population was majority Catholic.

The pursuit of legal remedies to this situation had proven fruitless, since the judiciary was almost exclusively Unionist. Consequently, in the 1960s the Catholic minority adopted the approach of the African American civil rights movement in the United States. The **Northern Ireland Civil Rights Association** (NICRA), a loosely consolidated grouping of Catholic nationalists, labor activists, student radicals, and sympathetic Protestants, emerged in 1967. Appropriately, its first demonstration involved a housing dispute in County Tyrone, where a Catholic Nationalist member of Parliament, Austin Currie, took over a house that he believed had been unfairly allotted to the young Protestant fiancée of a member of the security forces. The civil rights protest march in support of Currie's action set the template for future protests. As the 4,000 civil rights activists marched and sang "We Shall Overcome," they encountered vitriolic counterprotests from the more extreme Unionist factions. On that occasion, the marchers met with no physical violence. But in October 1968 when a civil rights protest in Derry/Londonderry proceeded despite being officially banned, mayhem resulted. The Royal Ulster Constabulary (the Protestant-dominated police force in Northern Ireland) employed brutal force against the marchers. The television footage of police battering unarmed protesters with batons and drenching them with water cannons shocked audiences in Ireland and Britain.

The **Northern Ireland Civil Rights Association** and movement attempted to use nonviolent tactics such as the marches they had seen in the United States earlier in the decade to press for reform in Northern Ireland in 1968–69.

Most Unionists regarded the protestors less as civil rights activists than as a front for militant Irish nationalism. The proclaimed agenda of the NICRA and its allies focused on basic reforms to the Northern Irish state—fair housing and employment, an end to the limits on suffrage and to gerrymandering, and removal of the Special Powers Act, which allowed the security forces to act with impunity. But the Unionist community believed that lurking behind these reformist proposals was the familiar specter of the nationalist quest for a united Ireland. Such fears were long-standing. The Unionists looked south to the Republic of Ireland and saw a state that in their eyes had merged its national identity with an authoritarian Catholicism, casting adrift southern Protestants and leading many of them to emigrate. Britain served as bulwark safeguarding Northern Ireland from the persistent threat posed by the Republic of Ireland, whose constitution laid claim to the entire island. Unionists, as the name implies, identified themselves and their state as British, but like an anxious lover, they were never sure that their deep feelings of attachment were reciprocated. From the outset of Northern Ireland's creation, Unionists worried that the British would eventually abandon them. Their survival, they believed, depended upon their steadfast commitment to maintaining power and preventing an unruly Catholic Nationalist minority from usurping it.

As the civil rights movement started in Northern Ireland, this Unionist consensus began to fracture, however slightly. A new UUP prime minister, Terrance O'Neill (1963–69), deviated from his predecessors. He displayed a modicum of respect for the Catholic minority, even going so far as to attend a Catholic service, and proposed some modest structural reforms to the Northern Irish state. While these fell far short of what the civil rights movement called for, especially in the area of electoral reform, where the demand for "one man, one vote" was ignored, they triggered alarm among hard-core Unionists. The most prominent of O'Neill's opponents was an evangelical preacher who appeared on the political scene in the 1950s. The Reverend Ian Paisley was a charismatic speaker who interfused mainstream Unionism with a fervid blend of fundamentalist theology and anti-Catholic bigotry. In a characteristic speech in 1969, he proclaimed that Catholics "breed like rabbits and multiply like vermin."[22] He regarded even the slight gestures of rapprochement that O'Neill made to the Catholic minority as a betrayal.

To counter O'Neillism, Paisley created the Ulster Constitution Defence Committee (UCDC), which in turn spun off the paramilitary group the Ulster Protestant Volunteers (UPV). The UPV adopted the same motto as the Ulster Volunteer Force (UVF), which itself was revived in 1966, "For God and Ulster." The UVF linked itself to the **Loyalist** organization originally founded during the Home Rule crisis of 1912–13 to prevent Protestant-dominated Ulster from being swallowed up by the rising tide of Irish nationalism. This new version of the UVF was a more ramshackle, less-disciplined group whose first actions involved the bombing of key infrastructure. (As was his habit throughout the Troubles, Paisley denied any direct knowledge or control of violent actions carried out by the UPV or UVF.) By misdirecting blame for the bombings toward the IRA, they hoped to undermine O'Neill's more moderate Unionism. The UVF also carried out sectarian murders of Catholics that they saw as fair retribution for IRA killings of Protestants.

Loyalist paramilitary groups, such as the Ulster Protestant Volunteers (UPV), Ulster Volunteer Force (UVF), and Ulster Defence Association (UDA), vied with each other for influence over Protestant areas but were united in their willingness to use violence to oppose Nationalists. They saw civil rights marches as cover for Republicans who wanted to destroy Northern Ireland.

Paisley's agitation inspired his followers in the UCDC/UPV to carry out a series of attacks on civil rights marchers, as when hundreds of UPV members confronted a march to Dungannon in October 1968. These actions culminated in a vicious attack on civil rights marchers in January 1969 at Burntollet Bridge outside Derry/Londonderry. A few hundred student activists from the group People's Democracy—led by, among others, Bernadette Devlin, the radical firebrand who would become the public face of this movement—had orchestrated a march across Northern Ireland. At Burntollet, as they approached their destination, the protestors encountered the RUC, its auxiliary the B Specials, and Loyalist paramilitaries, who greeted them with a barrage of rocks and then beat them with clubs and iron bars. When the battered group of protesters entered the city, the metamorphosis of a civil rights struggle into a sectarian conflict was complete.

By the summer of 1969, O'Neill was out of office. As his successor, James Chichester-Clark, attempted to shore up the tottering edifice of the Unionist state, rioting intensified throughout Northern Ireland, especially in the main cities of Belfast and Derry/Londonderry. The climax occurred during a traditional Protestant march on 12 August celebrating the actions of the Apprentice Boys, who thwarted the forces of the Catholic King James II from conquering Derry/Londonderry in 1688. The resulting riot quickly became a pitched battle between Protestants, the RUC, and Catholics centered in the Catholic ghetto known as the Bogside. The "Battle of the Bogside," as it became known, was soon outmatched by what happened in Belfast on 14 and 15 August. There angry crowds of militant Loyalists burned the homes of Catholics living in or near Protestant neighborhoods. By the time the riot was over, almost 2,000 families, 80 percent of them Catholic, had been driven from their homes. Exhausted and unable to contain the spread of violence, the RUC was replaced by British troops. Surprisingly, many of the Catholics of Belfast initially welcomed the arrival of the British military, regarding them as a more effective and equitable protector of the minority population than the RUC. In the past the role of defender had been performed by the Irish Republican Army, but that group was woefully unprepared for the August attacks. Having shifted from militant nationalism to a more politically oriented Marxism, the IRA lacked the discipline and arms necessary to defend the Catholics in Belfast, a failure registered in graffiti proclaiming that IRA stood for I Ran Away.[23]

This debacle resulted in a dramatic restructuring of the IRA. By the end of 1969, a new group calling itself the **Provisional Irish Republican Army (PIRA)** had emerged. The Provos, as they were called, sought to restore the organization to its roots, forgoing politics in favor of armed struggle for a united Ireland. (Since the PIRA became the dominant branch of the movement, we will continue to refer to them in this text simply as the IRA.) From their perspective, the reforms that followed in the aftermath of the August riots were inadequate. The disarmament of the RUC; the reformation of the hyperaggressive B Specials into a more disciplined military unit, the Ulster Defence Regiment; the establishment of a commissioner to hear housing complaints; the implementation of "one man, one vote": all of these steps by the government in Northern Ireland, especially the last, addressed concerns that were at the heart of the civil rights movement. But for the newly refashioned IRA, nothing less than the expulsion of the British and the establishment of a united Ireland was now acceptable, and thus they reconnected to the demands of the cultural nationalists across the twentieth century.

They wasted little time in pursuing those goals, inaugurating a bombing campaign against security forces and economic targets. But it took the actions of the British military to generate significant support for the IRA among the nationalist community.

The **Provisional Irish Republican Army (PIRA)** broke away from the official IRA in 1969 in order to defend Catholic communities against Loyalist attacks and to resume the war to drive the British out of Ireland. It soon became the dominant faction among Republicans and so we refer to it in the text as just the IRA.

In July 1970, a curfew was imposed upon Catholic neighborhoods in Belfast: 20,000 people were ordered to remain inside while the army conducted a search for weapons. The massive ransacking of their homes during this search restored the British military to its familiar role as oppressor in the eyes of the Catholic minority. Matters became even worse a year later when the new Unionist prime minister, Brian Faulkner, convinced the British that the worsening security situation required drastic measures. Operation Demetrius, the rounding up and internment without trial of suspected paramilitaries, began in August 1971. Over the next six months, 2,400 individuals were detained on the suspicion that they were members of the IRA. (No Loyalist paramilitaries were included in this initial phase of internment, and in fact the largest Loyalist paramilitary group, the UDA, was only formed in September 1971, although it often carried out violent activities under the cover name Ulster Freedom Fighters). While under detention, some of the prisoners suspected of IRA membership were subjected to beating, hooding, blaring "white" noise, sleep and food deprivation, and other forms of what has come to be known euphemistically as "enhanced interrogation techniques."[24] Not surprisingly, this policy backfired badly. Instead of decreasing sectarian violence, internment inaugurated the bloodiest period in the Troubles. It also resulted in a flood of new recruits to the IRA.

The growing animosity between the British army

and the Catholic minority in Northern Ireland exploded during an anti-internment protest march in Derry/Londonderry on 30 January 1972. In response to the usual rock-throwing that occurred on the fringes of these marches, a unit of British paratroopers opened fire on an unarmed crowd of protesters, killing fourteen (thirteen that day plus one who later died in hospital). **Bloody Sunday**, as the event became known, unleashed fury throughout Ireland. In Dublin, an angry crowd set fire to the British Embassy. Throughout Northern Ireland, sectarian violence spiked, making 1972 the bloodiest year of the Troubles, with more than 10 percent of the overall death toll occurring then. Not everyone responded with violence. A week after Bloody Sunday, a crowd of 100,000, including both Catholics and Protestants from Northern Ireland and elsewhere, marched in the border town of Newry to demand justice for the victims in Derry and to appeal for a peaceful resolution of the conflict. These voices were drowned out by the IRA bombs that now exploded with regularity throughout Belfast and that reached a crescendo on Friday, 21 July. On what became known as Bloody Friday, the IRA set off twenty-six bombs strategically placed throughout the center of Belfast to maximize their impact, leaving eleven people dead and injuring 130, many severely.

Bloody Sunday, 30 January 1972, when the use of force by British troops resulted in the killing of fourteen Catholics during a peaceful protest march against internment in Derry/Londonderry, turned Nationalist sentiment against Britain and intensified the guerrilla war.

Direct Rule from Great Britain

In the midst of this period of accelerating sectarian violence, the British government took a momentous step. Frustrated with the Unionist resistance to reform and the increasing cost, both human and financial, that the conflict imposed upon Britain, British prime minister Edward Heath suspended the Parliament of Northern Ireland and instituted **direct rule** from London. While the devolved Northern Irish parliament at Stormont established in 1922 had always been subordinate to the British Parliament in Westminster with regards to international relations, it still had control over most internal policy decisions in Northern Ireland. With the imposition of direct rule, that was no longer the case. For the next twenty-five years (with the exception of a brief interlude of several months), Northern Ireland would be governed by a British secretary of state and administrative staff. The IRA and other nationalists welcomed the demise of the repressive Unionist-dominated Parliament at Stormont. They regarded its dissolution as the first step toward the inevitable unification of Ireland. Unionists, on the other hand, reacted with dismay. William Craig, whose Ulster Vanguard movement together with Ian Paisley's newly formed Democratic Unionist Party gave voice to hard-core Unionism, greeted the introduction of direct rule by inaugurating a two-day strike of 200,000 workers and a massive protest in Belfast. These served to warn Britain about the risk of not paying heed to Unionist concerns, a message that would be even more forcefully delivered two years later.

The British prime minister suspended the local government of Northern Ireland sitting at Stormont when it could not stop the increasing violence and in its place established **direct rule** by officials from Westminster (London). Attempts to achieve devolution (returning local government to Stormont) failed from 1972 to 1997, as the Troubles continued.

The British government saw direct rule as a stop-gap measure that would enable it to implement the reforms necessary to create a viable governmental structure in Northern Ireland. Once that was accomplished, the British governmental officials and military could be withdrawn. The British wasted no time in advancing these reforms. In March 1973, just a year after the establishment of direct rule, the British government presented a constitutional proposal for Northern Ireland that called for a legislative assembly elected through proportional voting and for an executive branch in which power would be shared between the major Unionist and Nationalist parties. This was supplemented by what came to be known as the Sunningdale Agreement, which endorsed the formation of a Council of Ireland primarily constituted by ministers drawn evenly from both the Republic of Ireland and Northern Ireland. Its purpose would be to coordinate policies on key economic and other issues.

These proposals were enthusiastically supported by the Social Democratic and Labor Party (SDLP), a constitutional nationalist party established in 1970 whose leadership was primarily drawn from the civil rights movement. Their reception among Unionists was considerably more mixed. The mainstream Ulster Unionist Party (UUP), led by Brian Faulkner, accepted the British proposals begrudgingly. In January 1974, they joined with the SDLP and the small nonsectarian Alliance Party of Northern Ireland (APNI) to form Northern Ireland's first power-sharing government. This experiment in reform was short-lived. Hard-line Unionists, led by William Craig and Ian Paisley, stridently opposed power-sharing and any affiliation between Northern Ireland and the Republic of Ireland. A new Loyalist group, the Ulster Workers' Council, backed by the largest Loyalist paramilitary organization, the Ulster Defence Association, initiated a work stoppage in May 1974 that shut down electricity, water, and other crucial aspects of Northern Ireland's infrastructure. After several futile attempts to break this strike, Faulkner resigned as prime minister and the power-sharing government collapsed. Northern Ireland was again placed under direct rule from Britain and remained so when the multiparty peace talks began in 1996.

Over the next two decades, the British continued to pursue political solutions to the conflict in Northern Ireland. They organized a constitutional convention and held secret meetings with the IRA, but these made no real headway toward the goal of a peaceful resolution. The repression of the civil rights movement by the RUC and Loyalist militias followed by the reintroduction of British troops onto the streets of Northern Ireland and their use of violence against Catholics confirmed the real nature of the contest in the eyes of the Republican hardliners—a bitter battle to defend their community and render the North so costly to the British that they would leave. Thus, the sectarian violence continued to exact its brutal toll, not only in Northern Ireland but also in the Republic of Ireland and Britain. On 17 May 1974, at the outset of their strike, Loyalist paramilitaries set off bombs in Dublin and Monaghan in the Republic that killed thirty-three people, the highest death toll of any single day throughout the Troubles. The IRA responded the next fall by bombing a series of pubs in Birmingham and elsewhere in England, resulting in twenty-one deaths and 200 injuries.

TIP Consult the prologue and Section A of the core texts to find personal stories of those caught up in the violence.

As sensational as these bombings were, it was the unintended deaths of three children on the streets of Belfast in August 1976 that for a while seemed capable of halting the conflict. When an IRA getaway car whose driver was killed by police gunfire ran over three young children, one a six-month-old baby, it shocked the entire community of Northern Ireland. The outrage was quickly channeled into a peace movement. Throughout that August and September, the Peace People, founded by Betty Williams and Mairead Corrigan, held rallies in Belfast and throughout Northern Ireland in which tens of thousands of Catholics and Protestants came together to demand an immediate end to violence. Williams and Corrigan won the Nobel Peace Prize in 1977, but they could not overcome the divisions between the Unionist and Nationalist communities. Their appeal failed to persuade the paramilitaries on either side. The IRA and its sympathizers insisted that the armed struggle must continue until the British, whom they saw as the real cause of the violence, were driven out of Ireland. The UVF and UDA also were determined to continue to use any means to protect the Protestant community from what they saw as sectarian violence by the IRA.

Changing Strategies: Ulsterization, Criminalization, and the Hunger Strikes

In the aftermath of the failure of the Sunningdale Agreement, the British changed strategies. They abandoned the search for a large-scale political solution in favor of a narrower, more pragmatic approach to the sectarian violence. Their new policy of "Ulsterization" shifted the burden of dealing with the IRA from the British army to the RUC and its auxiliary force, the Ulster Defence Regiment (UDR).[25] The conflict was no longer treated as a war against a guerrilla army pursuing national liberation but as a law-and-order issue. The IRA (and, to a lesser degree, Loyalist paramilitaries) were cast as criminals. The new approach, with its emphasis on the systematic collection of evidence and confessions coerced from rigorous police interrogations, proved remarkably effective. But it also generated a drastic response that ultimately undermined its success. As a result of the policy of criminalization, IRA prisoners were no longer granted special status, no longer treated like political prisoners who could wear their own clothes and organize their own activities. Instead, they were given prison uniforms and assigned the same menial duties as ordinary criminals. From the outset, the IRA prisoners resisted this new regime, insisting that they were political prisoners and wrapping themselves in **blankets** instead of donning the prison uniform of an ordinary criminal. This eventually evolved into the more gruesome **"dirty protest,"** whereby the prisoners refused to leave their cells, which soon become excrement-covered hellholes.

When the British determined to treat IRA prisoners as criminals instead of prisoners of war, the prisoners responded by refusing to wear prison clothing and covering themselves with the **blankets** provided with their bedding. This escalated to the **dirty protest** when the blanket men refused to leave their cells, and eventually led to the **hunger strikes** in 1980–81.

The prisoners upped the ante again in 1980 by declaring a hunger strike until their "special status" as political prisoners was restored. Their demands were rebuffed by the new British prime minister Margaret Thatcher. Angered by the IRA's recent assassinations of prominent British figures, including most notably Lord Mountbatten, the queen's cousin and former viceroy of India, Thatcher refused to budge. She insisted that "the government will never concede political status to the hunger strikers or to any others convicted of criminal offences."[26] Poorly planned, this first hunger strike ended abruptly without any deaths. That was not the case with the one that began several months later on 1 March 1981. It was carefully orchestrated to generate maximum publicity, with a new prisoner joining the strike every two weeks so that the deaths would recur in agonizing succession. **Bobby Sands**, the first of the strikers, epitomized the image of martyrdom that the prisoners wanted to project. Young, photogenic, devoutly Catholic, he had been arrested for possessing a gun rather than for the violent acts usually associated with the IRA. By the time he died of starvation in early May, he was known throughout the world. This gruesome ritual of self-sacrifice continued throughout the next few months with nine more prisoners dying. Eventually, the families of the hunger strikers intervened and brought the strike to an end. Margaret Thatcher had won the battle with the IRA prisoners, but she lost the propaganda war.

Sinn Féin's tactic of running **Bobby Sands** for Parliament as he was dying on a hunger strike in prison expanded support for Republicanism and proved that Sinn Féin could succeed by running candidates in Northern Irish elections, even though they refused to take their seats once elected. Sands received more than 30,000 votes in his district, and over 100,000 people attended his funeral.

The hunger strike bolstered the reputation of the IRA, at a low ebb in the aftermath of several particularly barbarous attacks, most notoriously the firebombing of the La Mon Hotel near Belfast, which left twelve Protestant civilians dead. Even more significant, the strike presented the IRA with an unforeseen opportunity. Gerry Adams, widely acknowledged as its leader, had been eager to supplement the organization's armed struggle with a stronger political presence. So when a Northern Ireland seat for the British Parliament unexpectedly became open in the midst of Bobby Sands's hunger strike, Adams and others in the IRA leadership decided to run the charismatic Sands as a candidate for Sinn Féin, the political party affiliated with the IRA, while he was still in prison. Sands's victory in this nationalist district of Northern Ireland was merely symbolic. The Irish Republican leadership of the IRA and Sinn Féin had long abstained from holding elective office. They insisted that the last legitimate legislative body in Ireland had been the Dáil (the Irish parliament) that had preceded the island's partition in 1922. But Sands's election demonstrated that Sinn Féin could succeed electorally. That realization transformed the basic framework of the conflict in Northern Ireland.

This dramatic shift in the IRA's attitude toward electoral politics was heralded by Danny Morrison, one of Adams's top aides, when he addressed a Sinn Féin conference three weeks after the hunger strikes ended: "Who here really believes we can win the war through the ballot box? But will anyone here object if, with a ballot box in one hand and the Armalite [the automatic rifle used by the IRA] in the other, we take power in Ireland?"[27] Sinn Féin soon began contesting local council and parliamentary elections. When Gerry Adams won a parliamentary seat in the general election of 1983, it shocked the establishment. The fact that he was elected even though voters knew that he would refuse to take his seat in the British Parliament in Westminster made his victory all the more startling.

The rise of Sinn Féin as a viable political party caught the attention of the Irish taoiseach (prime minister), Garrett Fitzgerald. Afraid that Sinn Féin would become the dominant nationalist party in Northern Ireland, Fitzgerald sought to bolster the reputation of its counterpart, the more moderate SDLP. Even before Adams's election, Fitzgerald had announced the convening of the New Ireland Forum, a gathering of the main nationalist parties from the Republic of Ireland and from Northern Ireland (excluding Sinn Féin because of its presumed ties to the IRA) to fashion a solution to the conflict in the North. After a year of meetings, in which the SDLP's leader, John Hume, played a prominent role, the forum presented its conclusions. The report, issued in May 1984, proposed three options for the future of Northern Ireland: join with the Republic of Ireland to form a united Ireland; remain a separate state but enter into a confederation with the Republic of Ireland; be governed under the joint authority of the Republic of Ireland and Britain. The British prime minister, Margaret Thatcher, responded with disdain to these proposals, renouncing each one with a terse "That is out."[28] But despite the cursory rejection of its proposals, the New Ireland Forum served as a catalyst for extended negotiations between the Republic of Ireland and Britain. These culminated in the Anglo-Irish Agreement of 1985, a crucial stepping-stone on the pathway to peace.

Anglo-Irish Connections and the Opening to Negotiations

Neither the guns nor the bombs were silent during this period of negotiations. In 1984, two of the primary antagonists in the conflict, Gerry Adams and Margaret Thatcher, were almost killed in sectarian attacks. A Loyalist paramilitary group shot Adams three times in an assassination attempt, while an IRA bomb at a Conservative Party conference in Brighton killed five people and narrowly missed Thatcher. It was her unwillingness "to tolerate a situation of continuing violence" that led Thatcher to support the **1985 Anglo-Irish Agreement**.[29] At one level, the Anglo-Irish Agreement simply enshrined in a formal treaty the long-accepted premise that any change in the status of Northern Ireland would require the consent of the majority of its population. But it broke significant new ground in acknowledging "the rights and identities" of the two sectarian traditions, Nationalist and Unionist, in Northern Ireland. As significant, and more surprising, it established an intergovernmental conference in which Britain and the

Republic of Ireland would deal jointly with political, legal, and security issues in Northern Ireland. This inclusion of the Republic of Ireland in policymaking for Northern Ireland was a stunning departure on the part of the British, who had in the past consistently warned the Irish government not to interfere in the internal affairs of another sovereign state.

The Anglo-Irish Agreement of 1985 for the first time created an intergovernmental conference to allow consultation on Northern Ireland between Great Britain and the Republic of Ireland. It was angrily opposed by most Unionists, including the UUP and DUP.

The Anglo-Irish Agreement struck the Unionist community like an earthquake, shaking the foundations of their identity. For the first time in their history, the Unionists were not allowed to veto a policy that threatened their dominance. They responded with fury. Margaret Thatcher, previously regarded as a hero for her staunch refusal to bend to IRA demands, was now vilified. During a sermon, Ian Paisley called for God to "take vengeance upon this wicked, treacherous, lying woman."[30] The agreement was denounced by Unionist politicians and protested in the Protestant neighborhoods of Belfast. When the RUC attempted to restore order, they were attacked and threatened by those who had once been their strongest supporters. Loyalist paramilitaries demonstrated their displeasure by intensifying their killing of Catholic civilians. But the agreement stood. It served notice that the British government was willing to override Unionist concerns to bring about a peaceful resolution of the conflict.

If the Anglo-Irish Agreement enraged Unionists, it disconcerted the IRA and Sinn Féin. The agreement made it more difficult to justify their armed struggle by claiming that Britain was a colonial power determined to maintain its dominance over Northern Ireland. Having taken the dramatic step of ending its abstention from the Dáil, the Irish Republican leadership worried that this new context of Anglo-Irish cooperation would impair Sinn Féin's electoral prospects. They had other concerns as well. The British Special Air Service Regiment used information gleaned from informers to set up a series of ambushes. The most effective of these resulted in the killing of eight of the IRA's top operatives. But as happened so often in the past, it was the IRA's own actions that damaged it the most. On 8 November 1987, an IRA bomb exploded at a war memorial ceremony in the Protestant town of Enniskillen, killing eleven people and injuring sixty. This gratuitous slaughter of civilians devastated the IRA's reputation just as the republican movement was attempting to expand its political influence. It wasn't only the IRA whose actions generated controversy. In March 1988, British special forces killed three IRA operatives in Gibraltar, producing an international scandal for the manner in which the killings were conducted. The IRA members were unarmed, not given a chance to surrender peacefully, and, according to some witnesses, shot while prone on the ground.[31] As happened so often throughout the Troubles, one atrocity sparked another. When the two men and woman killed at Gibraltar were given a traditional IRA military burial at the Milltown cemetery outside Belfast, the large crowd that had gathered was attacked by Michael Stone, a solitary Loyalist paramilitary, who fired an automatic rifle and hurled grenades, killing several mourners. At the burial of one of these victims, two British soldiers inadvertently turned into the midst of the funeral procession. They were pulled from their vehicle, mercilessly beaten, and eventually shot.

Having opened an avenue to peace with the Anglo-Irish Agreement, the British hesitated to move forward. The ferocity of Unionist opposition to the agreement gave them cold feet. In particular, they resisted granting the Inter-governmental Conference the comprehensive authority envisioned in the agreement, restricting its focus primarily to security matters. What had seemed a direct path to peace negotiations branched into an array of talks—some discreet, some open. The British government began backchannel negotiations with the IRA while at the same time convening formal meetings of the key parties. But it was the secret discussions that John Hume, the leader of SDLP, initiated in 1988 with Gerry Adams that were to be the most significant. Despite his disgust with the IRA, Hume realized that there could be no meaningful peace settlement without their involvement, so he set about trying to convince Adams to end the IRA's armed struggle. With this in mind, Hume persuaded the British secretary for Northern Ireland, Peter Brook, to announce in 1990 that Britain had "no strategic or economic interest" in Northern Ireland.[32] Hume capitalized on this by working behind the scenes to get the British and Irish governments to make a formal statement reiterating Brook's position and acknowledging the right of the Irish people to self-determination. The **Downing Street Declaration** (see core text no. 16) issued jointly by the British and Irish governments in December 1993, included both the renunciation of British interest and the recognition of the right of self-determination that Hume had emphasized, but it augmented the latter by insisting that "the democratic right of self-determination by the people of Ireland" requires the "agreement and consent of a majority of the people of Northern Ireland."

The **Downing Street Declaration** in 1993 was a joint statement by the governments of Britain and Ireland recognizing the right of self-determination for the people of Ireland and the principle of consent for Northern Ireland. The hardliners on both side—DUP and Sinn Féin—rejected the declaration or demanded clarifications, but it was cautiously accepted by moderates.

The declaration also demanded "a commitment to exclusively peaceful methods" as a prerequisite for engaging in negotiations with the two governments. That last point was all too relevant, as sectarian violence had once again exploded; October 1993 was the bloodiest month of the Troubles since 1976.

The Sinn Féin leadership found the Downing Street Declaration unsatisfactory. They saw its linking of self-determination to the consent of the majority in Northern Ireland as restoring the power of the Unionist veto. But they had already invested themselves deeply in the peace process. Prodded by the Irish government and Irish American politicians, the IRA declared a ceasefire on 31 August 1994. Two months later, the major Loyalist paramilitaries followed the IRA's example and declared their own ceasefire. Peace talks seemed imminent, but once again the British hesitated. The Unionists doubted the authenticity of the IRA's ceasefire and demanded the **decommissioning** (the verified destruction) of IRA weapons as a precondition for Sinn Féin's participation in the talks. To placate the Unionists, the British government agreed.

Decommissioning was the demand that the IRA dispose of its weapons before Sinn Féin would be allowed to participate in public talks.

TIP Consult the core texts for the positions of the main parties involved in the talks: Section E for the Unionists and Section F for the Nationalists.

The delay caused by the debate over decommissioning frustrated the IRA and Sinn Féin. To protest what they regarded as foot-dragging, they took a dramatic step. On 6 February 1996, the IRA ended its ceasefire by setting off a massive bomb in the Canary Wharf district of London, killing two people and causing 100 million pounds in damage. The Irish and British governments were undeterred. Three weeks later, they announced that **multiparty peace talks** would begin in June 1996. This would be preceded by an election to determine each party's representation in the negotiations. When the talks began at Stormont on 10 June, they were chaired by the American diplomat and former senator George Mitchell, a choice sanctioned by both the Irish and British governments. Sinn Féin would not be allowed to participate until it demonstrated unequivocally its commitment to a nonviolent democratic process.

> **Multiparty peace talks** on the future of Northern Ireland at Stormont were initiated by the British government of Prime Minister John Major in 1996 and continued by the newly elected prime minister, Tony Blair, in 1997. Section D of the core texts contains the documents used to initiate the talks.

The positions of some members of the two competing sectarian communities were hardened by the experience of the Troubles. Hatred and bigotry toward the other side persisted among both Catholic Nationalists and Protestant Unionists. Most Unionists continued to reject Nationalist arguments that Ireland holds only one national community and insisted that their nationality was British not Irish. They were suspicious of negotiations with those who had denied their identity and engaged in terrorism against them. In a speech to the Democratic Unionist Party (DUP) annual conference, held shortly after the IRA's ceasefire, party leader Ian Paisley gave voice to the attitudes of a sizeable portion of the Protestant population when he condemned his Unionist counterparts for their negotiations with the IRA. In his mind and in those of many of his followers, such a process would inevitably lead to a reunification of Ireland. He described such a prospect with typical anti-Catholic vitriol, insisting that it would render northern Protestants "slaves in a country fit only for Nuns men and Monks women to live in" (see core text no. 21).

Some Nationalists continued to believe that the entire territory of Ireland should be united in one independent nation under the principle of national self-determination, a principle they saw as approved by the Irish people when Sinn Féin overwhelmingly won the parliamentary elections of 1918, the last all-Ireland election. They blamed the continued partition of Ireland on the British, whom these Nationalists thought wished to retain a strategic position on the island and were reluctant to confront the Unionists. They feared that the IRA ceasefire foreshadowed an abandonment of its ideals, that if the subsequent negotiations did not lead to the removal of any British presence and the reunification of Ireland, it would be a betrayal. Without the attainment of these goals, all the sacrifices endured during the Troubles seemed a waste. Some IRA combatants, believing the justification for their violent actions was being abandoned, suffered traumatic moral anguish.

Such trauma was not restricted to paramilitary operatives and British soldiers. The Troubles resulted in 40,000 casualties, more than 3,600 of whom were killed. In a small country like Northern Ireland, such losses touched a large portion of the population. As discussed above, the psychological damage triggered by this violence extended to the relatives, friends, and neighbors of the victims. This pervasive trauma fueled suspicion and sometimes hatred of one's sectarian opponents. It posed a significant roadblock to the attainment of a peace agreement.

Others, however, were willing to move forward despite the trauma they and their communities had endured. Those who supported the SDLP rejected the use of violence and recognized that even if the British left Northern Ireland, the Nationalists would still have to deal with the interests and concerns of the Unionist community. Some Unionists also understood that for Northern Ireland to escape its cycle of violence and poverty, they needed to recognize the legitimate interests of the Nationalist community and find some path to working together. Organizations, albeit still small, such as the Alliance Party and the Northern Ireland Women's Coalition, attempted to bridge the differences between the two sectarian communities, recognizing that any political solution must take account of the competing concepts of national community. While some members of the paramilitaries claimed the violence had been necessary to force their opponents to the negotiating table, in the leaders of the political parties most linked to the paramilitaries, such as Sinn Féin and the Progressive Unionist Party, there was a growing recognition that violence had resulted in a bloody stalemate and that political compromise was essential to end the cycle of murder and revenge.

Does enough common ground exist for an agreement? Has the moment come when a majority of each community are open to compromise? Will it be possible to build a basis for trust and collaboration in any peace settlement? Or at least to guarantee to each community that it could protect its own vital interests in a new government? Are the two communities locked in a historic cultural and ethnic conflict, permanently divided by their schooling, religion, marriages, fears, and desire for revenge after thirty years of violence; or is it possible that they can find a solution that recognizes the legitimate interests of each side and provides each a voice in a new constitutional arrangement?

The Current Moment, June 1997

During the first year, the multiparty talks bogged down in debates over procedural details. British prime minister John Major's government was hampered by its need for Unionist votes to maintain its majority in the House of Commons and thus was unwilling to make concessions to Sinn Féin on the issue of IRA decommissioning. The May 1997 elections in Great Britain gave the Labour Party a large majority in the House of Commons and thus provided Tony Blair, the new prime minister, the opportunity to make a renewed effort to reach an agreement. He named Mo Mowlam as secretary of state for Northern Ireland. Blair then visited Northern Ireland on 16 May and gave a speech that committed his government to the peace process laid out in the Downing Street Declaration, stating, "I am convinced that the time is right finally to put the past behind us and meet the deep thirst of the people of Northern Ireland for peace, normality and prosperity. My message is simple. I am committed to Northern Ireland. . . . But let us have no illusions. Commitment to democracy means no violence or threat of violence. There can be and will be no double standards."[33]

In June 1997, a similarly positive development occurred in the Republic of Ireland with the election of a Fianna Fáil coalition government led by Taoiseach Bertie Ahern. The previous Fine Gael taoiseach, John Burton, had antagonized Sinn Féin by supporting the British and Unionist position that IRA decommissioning was a prerequisite for Sinn Féin's participation in the multiparty talks. The IRA marked their displeasure with Burton's position by breaking their ceasefire with the Canary Wharf bombing. Taoiseach Ahern recognized the necessity of Sinn Féin's participation in the talks and rejected the idea of prior decommissioning as a requirement for that.

As the multiparty talks resume at Stormont, Sinn Féin is still barred from participating because the IRA has not declared a new ceasefire. The remaining parties still have to confront the issue of decommissioning and Sinn Féin's exclusion from the talks, as well as start to make substantive progress on the constitutional issues and the three strands set forth for discussion—Strand 1: relationships within Northern Ireland; Strand 2: relationships between Northern Ireland and the Republic of Ireland; and Strand 3: relationships between the governments of Great Britain and the Republic of Ireland. Time is running out. To succeed, those interested in peace will need to find a way to reconcile two competing visions of Northern Irish nationalism or at least find a way for each community to tolerate the other's participation in a common constitutional arrangement. Are there broader concepts of national identities that can provide new possibilities for agreement? Are there constitutional arrangements that can make sure that each national community feels equally secure, recognized, and expressed? If an agreement cannot be reached by the spring 1998, the whole process may fall apart, and the war will resume.

Issues to Be Debated in the Multiparty Talks

- *Decommissioning:* Should the paramilitaries (particularly the IRA) surrender their weapons before the talks can begin?
- *Constitutional issues:* What is the national identity of Northern Ireland? Is it to remain as part of the United Kingdom or be united with the Republic of Ireland? Who will make that decision?
- *Strand 1:* What will be the structure of a devolved government in Northern Ireland? Will it be subject to majority rule or provide a form of power-sharing? How will fairness between the two

communities be protected? (Internal relations within Northern-Ireland.)
- *Strand 2:* What will be the relationship between any government in Northern Ireland and the Republic of Ireland? Will the Republic play any role in determining internal policies in Northern Ireland? (North-South external relations.)
- *Strand 3:* What will be the relationship between Great Britain and the Republic of Ireland in consulting on conditions in Northern Ireland? (East-West external relations.)

3
The Game

MAJOR ISSUES FOR DEBATE

For over 100 years the status of the six counties in Northern Ireland has been the source of contention, violence, and political stalemate. It is difficult for outsiders to understand, particularly American students who often have a false image of Ireland framed around Saint Patrick's Day and movie stereotypes. There is some awareness that there is a conflict between Catholics and Protestants but little understanding that the conflict is less about theology than it is about ethnic and cultural issues rooted in economics, social status, political differences, and separate concepts of national identity. Understanding these larger issues is crucial to understanding the debates over the Troubles and their possible solutions, debates that are given all the more relevance by the resurgence of ethnic nationalism in the European Community and the United States in the last twenty years.

The Basic Questions: Nationalism and Democracy

Nationalism

What constitutes a national community? What factors create a common sense of belonging to one community as opposed to another? When faced with two communities with different national allegiances based on ethnicity, religion, culture, and historical experience, how do you reconcile them so that they can function together in one political system? Or must they remain divided? Is Ireland caught within the constraints of competing visions of cultural nationalism? Or are there forces within Ireland or outside it that could develop a broader concept of civic nationalism?

Democracy

Is democracy simply majority rule? What if historically the majority has discriminated against a minority and used tools such as gerrymandering and censorship to reduce the minority voice? How do you guarantee the equality of human and civil rights in a divided society? Can you maintain the principles of democracy while building a power-sharing system that provides some sense of protection to each community? Can you legislate cooperation and build trust? Or does power-sharing simply entrench permanently the divisions within the society?

Competing Ideas and Cultures
Religion

As outlined in the "Historical Background," there are three major religions in Northern Ireland—Roman Catholicism, the religion of all Irish before the sixteenth-century Reformation and the majority of native Irish after it; Anglicanism, created by Henry VIII's break with Rome and declaration of the king as head of the Church of England (1534) and then the Church of Ireland (1541), the religion of the landed and ruling classes in Ireland after the dynastic settlement of the Glorious Revolution (1688); and, finally, Presbyterianism (also known as the Dissenters in England; many later emigrated to the American colonies, where they were known as the Scotch-Irish), whose practitioners were brought from Scotland to settle in Ireland in the great Plantations of the seventeenth century. The theological distinctions among the churches were broadly rooted in the Catholic belief of the authority of scripture and church tradition, in an ordained priesthood to interpret the Bible and perform the sacraments, and its concept of salvation by faith and works versus the Protestant belief in salvation by faith alone, the authority of scripture alone, and the ability of the laity to read and interpret the Bible. Anglicanism developed a Protestant theology but maintained a hierarchical structure, while the Presbyterians emphasized predestination among the Protestant tenets, with the ability of each congregation to choose its own clergy and thus not be dependent on the authority of bishops.

Religion provided a lens through which individuals interpreted the world around them; a narrow lens since because of the segregation of the two communities, they had little interaction with or knowledge of the religions of the other community. The communities did not really debate theology or attempt to convert each other. Rather, religion became the fault line along which divisions in ethnic attachments, social and economic status, and political power were developed. Northern Ireland in the 1990s was still a highly segregated society. The primary and secondary levels of education were separated into Catholic schools and the state schools attended by most Protestants—only 2 percent of children attended integrated schools. Intermarriage was highly discouraged by both traditions, so a thicket of separate organizations grew up around schools and churches that provided segregated community interactions, social services, sports, and culture. Residential segregation in rural areas dated back to the Plantations, while in urban areas it had been worsened by the Troubles since 1968 and resulting "peace" walls built by the British army to separate the warring populations. This segregation was deepened by the economic troubles that in 1991 found 27.2 percent of Catholics unemployed versus 12.2 percent of Protestants, with Catholics actively discouraged from pursuing jobs in Protestant-dominated professions.[1]

Thus, by being born into a family of one religion or another, you were identified with a particular national community, and you had little opportunity to interact with people of a different religion. It was along these religious lines that each community built a cultural identity rooted in separate historical experiences. For the Catholic majority in Ireland as a whole, that identity was grounded in their lives in rural Ireland, in the repression of Catholic political and economic rights that resulted from the dynastic and religious wars of the seventeenth century, in the maintenance of an underground church, and in a long tradition of rebellion against British rule. For the Protestants in Northern Ireland, that identity was more urban and industrial by the nineteenth century, rooted in fear of the papist threats to the Crown of England and the Protestant faith, and a conviction of the threat that a backward-looking Irish Catholic culture represented to their liberal rights as British citizens and to the economic development of Ireland. These prejudices existed well into the later twentieth century.

For many of the young working-class men and

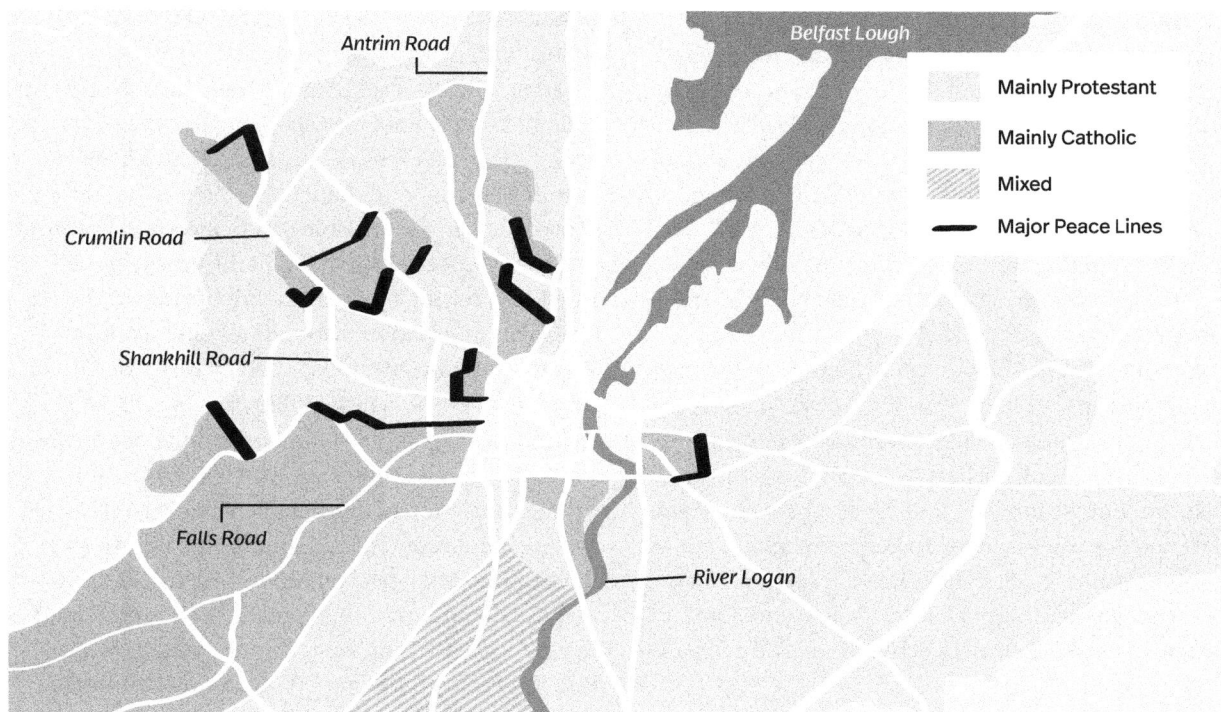

Distribution of religions in Belfast

women who were caught up in the Troubles in the 1970s and 1980s, the decision to join the fight was more basic—they were motivated to defend their own communities on a very personal level. They acted to protect their homes from being burned out by rioters; they joined paramilitaries for the chance to take revenge for murdered coreligionists and to defend their community against the other side's paramilitaries or the RUC and the British military. Later experience or education in the prisons might connect that basic instinct to defend their community to a larger political and historical understanding, or even, in the case of the IRA, to a sense of being part of a worldwide movement against colonial oppression. (Read section A of the core texts to better understand some of the personal experiences of participants in the Troubles.)

National Identity

Read again the discussion of the differences between civic nationalism and cultural nationalism in the introduction to the "Historical Background." As noted there, national consciousness is a broad feeling of belonging to one group as opposed to another. But political *nationalism* arises when that diffuse feeling is developed into an ideological movement. In taking the form of a sociopolitical movement, as noted by the scholar Anthony Smith, nationalists immerse themselves in the culture of the nation—rediscovering its language, history, literature crafted by the creation of journals, literary societies, academies, and cultural festivals. Intellectuals and cultural groups help to drive the development of shared national symbols, heroes, myths, and memories that define their community's values. Smith's definition of nationalism can help guide your research: nationalism is "an ideological movement for attaining and maintaining autonomy, unity and identity for a population which some of its members deem to constitute an actual or potential 'nation.'"[2]

Unionists should look to the concept of British civilization as defender of the rule of law, parliamentary government, and economic and scientific development that arose in the eighteenth and nineteenth centuries. The rituals and traditions created by the Orange Order, the Apprentice Boys, and similar Unionist groups reinforced for each new generation the values of the Protestant faith and the resistance to Rome rule. (Read particularly in section B of the core texts the statements on the "principles of loyalism" and the speeches by Ian Paisley, David Ervine, and David Trimble in section E.)

Nationalists should look to the literary and social academies and athletic clubs that strove to revive the Irish language and create a pantheon of ancient heroes to distinguish Irish civilization from English. Also mark how Sinn Féin and the IRA in each generation tied themselves to the history of rebellion and martyrs against British rule. (Read in section C of the core texts the writings of Patrick Pearse and Eamon de Valera as well as the speeches of Gerry Adams in section F.)

A basic sense of national identity does not dictate a certain type of political or social organization for a state. Scholars can identify multiple varieties of nationalism; for purposes of this game we have tried to organize the historical narrative to demonstrate the development of both *civic nationalism* and *cultural nationalism*.

Civic nationalism recognizes political identity is a matter of individual choice. Its proponents have as their object the making of a secular, representative state that will guarantee its members equal political rights within a government based on popular sovereignty where they as citizens participate in making the laws. Civic nationalism appeared in the revolt of the United Irishmen in the 1790s and in the concepts of some of the leading proponents of Home Rule at the end of the nineteenth century.

Cultural nationalism develops when a group forms an ethnic identity based on a common religion, language, traditions, and shared historical experience and then claims that as a separate national group with its own unique culture it has the right to assert its own political sovereignty without foreign interference. Instead of a matter of political choice, a person's national identity is determined by their birth and inheritance of an ethnic tradition.

Many scholars assert that the conflict in Northern Ireland is really about *competing concepts of cultural nationalism* that arose in the eighteenth and nineteenth centuries and then hardened into political movements in the crucible of rebellion and war from 1912 to 1922. Sections B and C of the core texts will provide you with a more in-depth portrait of the ways Unionists and Nationalists defined their communities. One identity was developed by the *Irish Nationalists*, who look to a united Republic of Ireland as their ultimate goal. The other communal identity was developed by the *Unionists*, who look to Great Britain for the protection of their political liberty, Protestant religion, and economic prosperity. The subsequent development of the Stormont regime in the North and the Republic of Ireland in the South reinforced the fears of each cultural community that it would lose its identity if subsumed into a state dominated by a majority of the opposing group. Moreover, it would not have the ability as a minority to guarantee that economic and political benefits are fairly distributed.

Ethnic and cultural identity is thus closely tied to the desire for political autonomy and the right of self-determination, and a national community can be frustrated if it is held in a subordinate position and suffers discrimination. It was fear of being placed under a Home Rule government made up predominantly of Catholic representatives that caused the Unionists led by Edward Carson to form the Ulster Volunteer Force in 1912 and threaten to use violence unless the six counties of Ulster were given their own devolved government—a demand acceded to by the British government in 1921. The government of Northern Ireland justified a regime that used gerrymandering to limit the voting power of Nationalists and deliberately discriminated in housing, education, and employment not just on the basis of religion but also on their assertion that the Catholics were treasonous. The Republican Easter Rising of 1916 and the subsequent war of Sinn Féin and the IRA against the British from 1919 to 1921 convinced Unionists that

Irish Nationalists were enemies of the United Kingdom. In their view nearly every Catholic was a Nationalist who was not just theologically in error but also a political traitor to the state.

For the Nationalists, the discrimination suffered at the hands of the Stormont government in Northern Ireland was experienced as an attempt to repress the legitimate political voice of the Nationalist community and thus represented another atrocity resulting from the long, illegitimate colonization of Ireland by the British monarchy.

Some Irish men and women asserted a more open and flexible concept of civic nationalism. Wolfe Tone and many of the United Irishmen who led a revolt against British Rule in 1798 had a multicultural concept of Irish nationalism that was based on individual liberty. They looked to the broad definitions of human rights, citizenship, and religious toleration that echoed from the American and French Revolutions. But their ambitions were frustrated by being caught between Britain's desire to protect its strategic military interests by controlling Ireland and the cultural divide between the urban Protestant elites and rural Catholic peasants that prevented a united action by the Irish community. The leaders of the Home Rule movement and the revival of Irish culture at the end of the nineteenth century were Protestant as well as Catholic, but the threat of violence brought forth by both the Unionists in 1912 and the Nationalists in 1916, coupled with Britain's blunders in handling the aftermath of the Easter Rising undermined any possibility of a peaceful constitutional settlement of the Irish problem across sectarian lines.

It is important to understand that each community became more wedded to the reading of history promoted by its most extreme elements and more willing to threaten to use violence because each saw violence not only as necessary to protect its communal interests but also as a successful tactic to force concessions from the British government.

Unionists expressed a siege mentality. Determined to defend their power against a treacherous Catholic majority in the whole of Ireland, they created a culture centered on the Orange Order and its bitter fear of the threat that Catholics posed to the Protestants in Ireland. That hostile view took root in the seventeenth-century dynastic battles and shaped Protestant interpretations of what they saw as the treasonous rebellions against the British state by Catholics in 1798 and 1916. Ultimately, it led Unionists to fear the establishment in the South of a Republic that was tied to the Catholic Church. The Unionists' threat from 1913 on to fight to defend their position compelled the British to carve out the six counties in Northern Ireland for partition in 1920. Unionists then continued to justify harsh and repressive measures against Catholics to protect their rule under the Stormont regime and during the Troubles.

Nationalists echoed Wolfe Tone's call to break the connection of Ireland with England, "the never-failing source of all our political evils," reaching from the seizure of land and penal laws in the seventeenth century, to the Great Famine and Irish emigration in the nineteenth century, and finally the rejection of Home Rule by the British Parliament in the decades before World War I. Many were determined to establish a separate culture rooted in the Irish language and separate Gaelic sports and cultural life. By the early twentieth century, they increasingly used a Catholic language invoking the example of Christ's blood sacrifice to justify violent action to establish and preserve an independent Irish Republic. Their use of guerrilla war led to the establishment of the Irish Free State after 1922, a state that explicitly tied itself to the values of the Catholic Church in its constitution of 1937 and maintained a claim over the six northern counties. Eire eventually left the British Commonwealth when it proclaimed a Republic in the twenty-six southern counties in 1948. The Provisional IRA in Northern Ireland continued to propagate the belief after 1970 that only self-sacrifice through armed struggle could keep the Republican vision alive and ultimately drive the British out of Northern Ireland as well, after witnessing the failure of the peaceful political efforts of the Irish civil rights movement.

Thus, in confronting the problem of Northern Ireland in the mid-1990s, *each participant must gauge and communicate the type of nationalism that is embraced by their own party* by consulting the documents in sections E and F of the core texts. You must determine your own vision for the future of Northern Ireland based on your role and the evidence. Then you must advocate for a political settlement that protects your concept of nationalism while accommodating the competing versions of national identity expressed by your opponents. Must the competing concepts of cultural nationalism be recognized, and a system built in which the two distinct traditions can share power? Or is it possible to build a consensus and political system based upon a broader cross-community concept of civic nationalism?

Concepts of Democracy

Each party must choose between three concepts of democracy in order to try to build a political system that can end the Troubles in Northern Ireland:

1. *Democracy based on majority rule*, in other words, that any decision on the future of Northern Ireland must be based on a simple majority of voters and that in parliamentary elections the party that wins the majority of seats should control the executive and appoint the ministers of government.
2. *Democracy of integration,* a belief that the government should not formally recognize separate ethnic or nationalist identities but challenge them and create cooperation through a more fluid and open concept of citizenship. It calls for rights based on individual citizenship, and not membership in an ethnic or cultural group, within a system in which all citizens are treated as equals and which eliminates discrimination in voting, housing, education, and employment. This form of settlement would need to develop a constituency for a broader civic nationalism and form structures to encourage cooperation among political parties and social interaction across sectarian lines, as well as provide incentives for parties that seek voters across both communities. It would promote intergroup communication and cooperation.
3. *Consociationalism* recognizes the existence of a basic mistrust between the two national communities. Proponents advocate a power-sharing structure within Northern Ireland drawn along the existing Unionist-Nationalist divide. The two communities would need to agree to a coalition in which they share power in both the legislative assembly and the executive based on proportional representation in which each representative or minister is clearly labeled as Unionist or Nationalist. But more than just guaranteed representation by Unionists and Nationalists, consociationalism would call for an exception to majority rule by providing for a "mutual veto" in which either community has the ability to veto any measure it sees as discriminatory and retains the right to autonomy in decisions on its own cultural affairs.

Those who argue for consociational power-sharing insist it is the only way to provide for collaboration between the major parties when such fundamental mistrust remains between them. For some, allowing a minority to block certain kinds of laws violates the principle of majority rule. Integrationists, in turn, would fear that building in protected seats and a mutual veto for each group would entrench those divisions permanently within the government and risk delaying or preventing a transformation of the society into one of mutual respect and dependence.

TERMINOLOGY AND POLITICAL OPTIONS

In the sources drawn from political speeches and news stories, key terms are often used interchangeably with overlapping meanings. However, to clarify the political issues for the purposes of this game we will hold to these definitions of key terms within the description of the game.

Key Terms Used in the Game

Self-determination: The claim that the people of Ireland as a whole have the sovereign right to determine their own form of government. This will frequently be joined to the concept that the people of Ireland have a separate ethnic and cultural identity from that of the United Kingdom.

Principle of consent: The claim that no change can be made to the status of Northern Ireland without the specific consent of the majority of the citizens within Northern Ireland itself (i.e., that the votes of the Protestant Northern Irish cannot be allowed to disappear in a vote of the Irish people as a whole, with the island's overwhelming Catholic majority).

Devolution: The transfer of authority over local government from the British Parliament in London to an elected legislature in Northern Ireland with its own executive. As a model, in the late twentieth century Britain gave various local powers to devolved governments in Scotland and Wales while retaining overall direction of foreign affairs and economic policy for the whole of the United Kingdom.

Majority rule: The claim that the internal government of Northern Ireland must be based on the democratic principle of majority rule. In the "first past the post" system used in the rest of Britain, the candidate with the plurality of votes in each district would win the election and the party with the most seats in the parliament would form the government. This could be seen as problematic if one community is permanently in the minority and thus loses most elections, particularly if the electoral districts are gerrymandered to spread the majority ethnic groups votes as broadly as possible while confining minorities within a few districts. In a proportional representational system, parties will be assigned a number of seats according to their proportion of the votes, providing them with a guaranteed voice but still potentially leaving minorities at a disadvantage in any assembly since they will still hold fewer seats than the majority parties.

Power-sharing/consociationalism: An arrangement that takes the concept of proportional representation further than in majority rule. It involves a *grand coalition*, in which all the main groups in the society (usually separate ethnic communities) are represented in government, thus in principle requiring them to cooperate and compromise; *proportionality*, in which all parties are represented in both the executive and legislative branches of government according to their proportion of the vote; *mutual veto*, in which each community of the society can veto any decision that its members believe is against their vital interests; and *segmental authority*, in which each community can make decisions on its own important cultural matters.

Integrative power-sharing: A practice that opposes building ethnic differences and conflict into the structure of the constitution and instead advocates building political, educational, and social institutions that transcend the differences, offering incentives for parties to appeal to all communities, and establishing a more inclusive democracy.

The Range of Options for a Political Solution[3]

Integration with Britain: Northern Ireland remains an integral part of the United Kingdom and is directly governed by the British Parliament at Westminster. The British political parties would organize and operate in Northern Ireland as they do in England, Scotland, and Wales. Northern Ireland would cease to have its own regional parties. Some Unionists favor this option as the best protection for their rights as British citizens, and indeed Northern Ireland has been under a form of direct rule from Great Britain since 1972.

Devolved government: A government is formed in Northern Ireland with the legislative powers to administer its own local affairs. (Typical government ministries would be Agriculture and Rural Development; Culture, Arts, and Leisure; Education; Employment, Enterprise, Trade, and Investment; Environment; Finance; Health, Social Services, and Public Safety; Regional Development; and/or Social Development. Foreign Policy and Defence would remain in the hands of the British government in Westminster.) This devolved government would be based on the principle of consent—the majority of the citizens of Northern Ireland would need to approve its political structure and policies. Many Unionists and some Nationalists favor this option as providing the people of Northern Ireland with some direct control over the administration of their government and local policies on taxation, education, housing, and economic development, and so on, rather than leaving them at the whims of ministers in London. Devolution could be based on majority rule as it was from 1921 to 1972, but reformist devolutionists—some Unionist and some Nationalists—insist that minorities need safeguards in any new government, including a bill of rights and proportional representation. Some would argue for a mandated power-sharing with a guaranteed role for minority parties within legislative committees and the administration (consociationalism). For some Nationalists, even power-sharing does not go far enough. They would assert that the government of the Irish Republic should have a significant role in any devolved administration in order to protect minority Catholic rights through North-South councils that make decisions of mutual interest to Northern Ireland and the Republic of Ireland.

Independent Northern Ireland: Some would argue that since neither British nor Irish sovereignty is acceptable to both major communities in Northern Ireland, it would be better for Northern Ireland to become independent. They have been challenged over whether an independent Northern Ireland would be too small to be economically viable.

Repartition: This would involve redrawing the borders of Northern Ireland to create two areas, one with a majority of Protestants and one with a majority of Catholics who could then govern their own nationality. One objection is that wherever the boundaries are drawn, it would still leave a minority of each religion on the wrong side of the border, in an area dominated by the opposing community.

Joint authority: This would require the United Kingdom and the Republic of Ireland to share sovereignty of Northern Ireland, determining policy on an equal basis. This appeals to some Nationalists; however, many Unionists would fear this would mean loss of the ability of the people of Northern Ireland to have a voice in laws that would be determined in Dublin and London, or, worse, that this would be a first step toward a united Ireland.

United Ireland: This choice would reunify the six counties of Northern Ireland with the remainder of the Republic of Ireland to form one thirty-two county state. Most Nationalists hold a long-term aspiration to see the island of Ireland reunified. For decades the IRA has tried and failed to force Britain to leave and to achieve reunification by violence and coercion. Such an outcome has been vigorously opposed by Unionists, and the Irish government has some trepidation about trying to govern a hostile Protestant minority that has been forced into reunification. However, is there some possibility of opening the door to unification by consent of a majority of the people of both Ireland and Northern Ireland? Would all parties and paramilitary groups need to renounce the use of violence in order to make this viable? Is there a possible agreement on the principle of consent that may not bring about unification in the short term but opens this possibility in the future?

Place these options in the context of the political guidelines that the British and Irish governments detailed in the documents in section D of the core texts. Note that in 1997 both the Republic of Ireland and Great Britain (and thus Northern Ireland) are members of the European Union. Does the larger project of the European Union in building a consensus on democratic government above separate ethnic and national identities provide models of citizenship that will be useful in your debates? Does the EU statement on human rights provide an umbrella under which to build a broader civic nationalism for both communities?

Ultimately, a majority of the parties in the multiparty talks will have to agree on the nature of the government of Northern Ireland and its relationship to Great Britain and the Republic. What is a common vision of the rights of citizens and nationalism that can draw the support of the majority of both the Unionist and Nationalist communities? What is the form of democracy that can safeguard rights and cultural identities yet force collaboration on parties that have long looked at each other as enemies? How will you build the trust necessary to the functioning of a culturally diverse democracy, in which neither side wants to be subservient to the other, even if guaranteed equal citizenship?

RULES AND PROCEDURES

The multiparty talks will operate under ground rules established by the British government in an official paper in March 1996 (core text no. 18): "The purpose of the negotiations will be to achieve a new beginning for relationships within Northern Ireland, among the people of the island of Ireland and between the peoples of these islands, and to agree new institutions and structures to take account of the totality of relationships."

As such the British government has appointed a chair for the talks, US senator George Mitchell (who will be joined by cochairs John de Chastelain and Harri Holkeri in larger games). Senator Mitchell will outline a basic agreement on democratic principles for all parties (core text no. 19). Within the context of the game, the participants will develop and vote on proposals to address the following issues and attempt to achieve a comprehensive peace settlement:

- Participation in the talks of political parties connected to paramilitary groups: Will participation of these parties be permitted if they merely declare a ceasefire, or will they be required to divest themselves of all weapons (decommission) before being allowed to participate?
- A proposal for a new government that will provide an agreement on the large constitutional issues noted above and offer detailed proposals for Strand 1: the political relationships and legislative and executive institutions within Northern Ireland; and Strand 2: the relationship within the whole of Ireland of the administration of Northern Ireland with the Republic of Ireland (North-South relations). The British and Irish representatives will develop a proposal for Strand 3: the relationship between the governments of Great Britain and the Republic of Ireland (East-West relations). Their proposal will be included in a final draft agreement to be debated and voted on by the members of the talks.

Chair

Senator George Mitchell will chair the talks; he does not vote. If Senator Mitchell is not present, one of his cochairs or, in a smaller game, the British representative will moderate. At the beginning of each session, the chair will verify that the paramilitary groups linked to the participating parties have continued to maintain a ceasefire. If anyone challenges the participation of any party, their continued presence will be put to a vote by the conference. Senator Mitchell may call for straw votes to determine if there is a consensus as the various strands are discussed. No vote is binding until the final vote on the whole agreement, at which time the agreement will need not only a majority of the votes in the whole conference but also majorities within each of the Nationalist and Unionist participants (see below, under "Voting").

As stated in the British rules for the talks (core text no. 18): "Any participant will be free to raise any aspect of the three relationships, including constitutional issues and any other matter which it considers relevant. While no outcome is either predetermined or excluded in advance, . . . *any agreement, if it is to command widespread support, will need to give adequate expression to the totality of all three relationships* [that is, the three strands]."

The Chair's Duties

- The chair will determine the specific agenda for each session as well as the order for considering any proposals or amendments. The chair may call a brief recess if needed at any point to consult with the representatives of the British and Irish governments on any unforeseen events or complications and/or to allow for faction meetings.
- The chair will set the rules for the debates, including the amount of time allotted for formal speeches and follow-up questions.
- Any member of the talks may make a formal speech or participate in the informal discussion. A podium will be provided for formal speeches, and any member who is not being recognized may also go to the podium, where she or he must be recognized by the chair within a short time. (The GM may remind the chair of this responsibility if necessary.)

Proposals and Debate

During the first meeting sessions of the multiparty talks, the discussions will be fairly open in order to produce an understanding of the main concepts and issues on the table. In the final session, debate will be tied to consideration of the draft agreement proposal drawn up by the chair with the intent to hold a formal vote by the participants. Once the draft proposal is on the table any participant may make formal proposals for amendments or modifications to the draft. These proposals should be presented in writing and will be discussed and voted upon in the order decided by the chair. If a proposal does not receive a second, it will be withdrawn. Proposals will have a greater chance of success if the delegates who initiate them have negotiated with other parties to support their position in advance of the formal meeting.

Voting

Approval of the individual proposals for the three strands and any amendments to them will require a majority vote of all parties that are authorized to participate in the talks. Each party will have one vote.

The final full agreement must be approved by a majority of all of the parties authorized to participate in the talks as well as a majority of both of the individual (self-identified) Unionist and Nationalist communities at the talks.

The chair and cochairs do not have a vote; every other representative, including the government representatives, at the talks has one vote. When tallying the results on the final agreement, the chair will track both the overall total from all the parties, and also the individual tallies of those individuals in the parties identified as Unionist (Ulster Unionist Party [UUP], Democratic Unionist Party [DUP], United Kingdom Unionist Party [UKUP], Progressive Unionist Party [PUP], and Ulster Democratic Party [UDP]) or Nationalist (SDLP and Sinn Féin). The final agreement will only be passed with both a 51 percent approval of the entire membership of the talks, and a 51 percent approval by each of the Unionist and Nationalist factions who are seated at the table (excluding those parties that have walked out). The agreement fails automatically if either the British or Irish representative votes no.

If the comprehensive peace proposal passes at the multiparty talks, the GM/instructor may instruct you to carry out a *referendum campaign* and vote for ratification of the agreement in Northern Ireland. The GM will explain the rules for the vote at that time.

Press Conferences and Public Opinion

If there are political parties that have been excluded from the talks or who have withdrawn from the talks, the chair will call a halt to each individual session with ten minutes remaining in class time to allow for press conferences. Any political parties not at the conference table must hold a press conference to provide their opinion on the issues debated within the session. (If no parties are excluded from the talks, the GM may cancel the press conferences to provide time for faction meetings.) The GM will ask if any other parties also wish to hold a press conference and designate areas of the classroom for each conference. Parties may feel free to hang posters and distribute position papers or press releases as part of the press conferences. Each party holding a press conference must first make a prepared statement on their reactions to the current issues under debate at the talks. Then they should be ready to entertain questions from the other participants in the talks.

All parties should be aware that their written essays, conference debates, or party statements have an impact on public opinion outside the conference room. They will be walking the tight rope of finding compromises while also maintaining the loyalty of their core supporters. (This reflects historical reality —although the content of the talks was supposed to be confidential, news of discussions there were quickly leaked by all parties in a battle to gain public support or to spark public outrage.) Failure to adequately address the concerns of their supporters (either to defend their original positions or to explain the need for compromises) may hurt the party when it appeals for support in the final public referendum on the agreement.

Marches

Parties that feel ignored or excluded by the multiparty talks may resort to unauthorized marches (in the classroom or outside it) to make their feelings known and express support for or opposition to the draft agreement. Marches have a deep history in Northern Ireland, from the Orange Order's annual marches and parades to celebrate past Protestant victories to the civil rights marches of the late 1960s imitating the tactics of Martin Luther King Jr. in the United States. Demonstrators should research public marches and posters in Northern Ireland in the 1990s to exhibit proper use of colors, symbols, and slogans for the demonstrations and accompany them with posters to hang in the classroom. Any party can initiate a march at any time, but no more than one march may take place in any class session. The chair may appeal to the police and British army (the GM) to control marches that are too disruptive or risk leading to violence. Demonstrators should be aware that public actions may risk retaliation by the police or paramilitary groups.

To initiate a march, the member(s) of the political party should stand, hold up a protest poster, and announce that they will hold a march. The GM will pause the proceedings in the conference and announce that attention will be turned to the streets where members of the parties who are conducting the march will present a speech, song, poem, or in any other appropriate way indicate the ideas they wish to convey. If the march becomes disruptive or opposing parties challenge the ideas being presented, the GM will consult an appropriate chart to reveal the consequences of the protest action. When the action is concluded, the GM will return the assembly to its debate, although the assembly should now be aware of the impact that its decisions may have outside of the meeting hall.

Visual and Written Imagery

All parties are encouraged to produce posters, slogans, poems, songs, or short videos that help to explain and defend their political positions to the larger voting public. For examples of the imagery used in Northern Ireland, see websites such as the CAIN Web Service, Examples of Posters 1968–1999, https://cain.ulster.ac.uk/images/posters/. The GM may also distribute examples of mural art from Northern Ireland that provides samples of the images used by each community. Consult with the GM for the best way to display your party's posters in the classroom or digitally.

Violence

Some of the parties present at the talks believed that war and the use of violence had been successful in forcing compromise on their opponents and causing them to seek a political solution. Although the major paramilitary groups and parties have agreed to the ceasefire, at any point in the proceedings the representatives at the talks may have to confront violent events that happen outside the talks. There are still small radical Loyalist and Republican paramilitary groups that have not declared ceasefires, and, of course, there is mistrust about the dedication to the peace process of the groups who have declared a ceasefire: the IRA, UVF, and UDA. If sectarian or political assassinations or bombings occur, the conference members may need to interrupt their regular debates to consider whether certain parties should be expelled for condoning violent acts. A majority vote for expulsion will force the designated party to withdraw from the talks for the remainder of the session.

Coalition Building

No single party is strong enough alone to dominate the talks; agreement can only be achieved through coalition building. Parties invested in achieving a final agreement must remember that they need to win the majority support of the representatives from both the Unionist and Nationalist communities for an agreement to be approved. Consult your role sheet for your relationship to the other factions and be prepared to negotiate with the other parties both inside and outside the regular sessions (through face-to-face or electronic means) in order to build support for your position. What positions are essential to protect your party and cultural community and on what issues may you be willing to compromise? Listen carefully to the hopes and concerns expressed by potential negotiating partners in order to find those areas where your views align, or where you may be willing to give up smaller goals in order to achieve your major objectives.

Assignments

Each participant will write at least two 1,500-word essays advocating for their positions and critiquing the position of opposition parties. These essays should present a clear claim, reasons the author advances the claim, and evidence for each reason drawn from sources presented in the game book and the student's additional research. Participants should consult their roles for more specific guidelines on the topics of their essays. In the standard schedule, the chair and the British and Irish representatives will write and send electronically their first essays to the GM before the start of Session 3 (the first meeting of the talks) and their second essays before the start of Session 5 (the third meeting of the talks). The rest of the participants will send their first essay to the GM before the start of Session 4 (the second meeting of the talks) and the second essay before the start of Session 6 (the fourth meeting of the talks). The timing and structure of the essays may be modified by the GM.

Objectives and Victory Conditions

You and the other representatives at the talks are attempting to find answers to the major questions under debate summarized above. Your individual objectives are found in your role sheets and you should consult them frequently during the game play. How do you define the national identity of Northern Ireland? What form of democracy has a chance of installing an effective government? In essence, the party that is able to place most of its victory objectives in the final agreement and then get the final agreement approved at the talks will win the game. Thus you will need to persuade others to approve an agreement that meets most of your objectives. But be aware of these important caveats:

- No one party alone can achieve victory—you will need to find allies.
- No one group—the Nationalists or the Unionists—can achieve victory alone, they must also get the majority of the other community to vote for the agreement.
- To create a broader coalition you will need to make effective arguments for your core beliefs but compromise on some issues may be necessary.
- All parties will have to determine how much they can compromise and still hold onto their core constituents—voters who they will need to win any citizen referendum on the agreement. Can you make an argument that the agreement that you negotiate ultimately helps to protect your national community?
- Some parties or individuals may conclude that blocking an agreement is the only way to protect their values; while others will lose absolutely if no agreement is reached. Carefully review your individual victory objectives, consult with any colleagues you may have within your party or national community, and ask the game master if you have any questions.

Although all politicians have an element of personal ambition, you are less motivated by personal ambition in this game than your broader goals of ending the war and establishing an effective government while protecting your own community and sense of national identity. It is important that you not only make a strong case for your own objectives but also listen carefully to the representatives of the governments and the other political parties in order to identify possibilities for compromise. Never forget that the broader population of Northern Ireland is observing your actions in an atmosphere rife with mistrust and with the potential to explode into violence.

Other Considerations and Advice

- The GM may periodically pass out news bulletins containing news of breaking events or reactions to actions taken at the talks. Some will be available to all players and some will be given to select individuals or groups. The participants in the multiparty talks should be prepared to react to external events that may impact the public perceptions of the talks and the chance for a peaceful settlement.
- The GM will represent important figures who are not present at the daily sessions of the talks, such as the British prime minister, the Irish taoiseach, and the president of the United States. If a participant wishes to communicate with one of these figures, they should approach the GM to find out the best means to do so.
- Along with their formal required essays, players will find it wise to distribute messages, draft proposals, petitions, poems, posters, or other writings to selected parties with whom they hope to form alliances, as well as to arrange for meetings outside of class time, in order to persuade them, plan strategy, or find ways to appeal to public opinion.
- While outside research can always help you understand the historical situation and your role and add depth and examples to your essays, you can find the materials that you need to succeed in the historical material and the core texts in the game book. *Master the relevant documents in the game book for your role first, then seek to understand the concerns of the other parties in order to search for common ground on which to build coalitions.* If you do conduct additional research, remember that you cannot refer to any event or cite any primary source that occurs after April 1998. If you aren't sure whether some data or information would have been available to your character in 1998, consult with the GM.

BASIC OUTLINE OF THE GAME

Below is a detailed schedule for the standard version of the game. Instructors have the option of choosing a shorter or more extended version of the game and will inform the class of any modification of the schedule as presented here.

Setup and Context Sessions
Session 1. Introduction to Reacting, Historical Background, and Broad Themes of the Game
Students should read parts of the historical background or sections of the core texts as assigned by the instructor. Particularly useful for an initial discussion could be reading the prologue and section A of the core texts. In this initial reading, try to understand the deep emotions attached to the identity of both the Unionist and Nationalist communities in Northern Ireland.

Session 2. Discussion on the Troubles
Students should review part 3 of the "Historical Background" chapter in order to understand the history of the Troubles and review the "Major Issues for Debate" section in "The Game" chapter. The instructor may administer an optional quiz on this material. Can you understand the causes of the Troubles in Northern Ireland and identify the historical roots of each community's sense of identity?

Game Begins
Session 3. First Meeting of the Multiparty Talks
All parties except Sinn Féin will participate in the session since at this point the Provisional IRA has gone back on its 1994 ceasefire. The chair will present the Mitchell Principles (core text no. 19) and ask each party to indicate its approval of them in order to remain in the talks. Any party that joins subsequent sessions must also first indicate its acceptance of the Mitchell Principles.

AGENDA
Item A: Decommissioning. Should the IRA be required to fully decommission its arms before Sinn Féin is allowed to participate in the talks? Should both a declaration of ceasefire and a full decommissioning of weapons be required of all paramilitary groups before the political talks begin? Is there an alternative to requiring full decommissioning?

Item B: Constitutional Issues. Parties should present their understanding of their own communities' national identity and their position on the overall constitutional position of Northern Ireland. Is it part of the Irish nation as a whole or is it a separate province with its own identity within the United Kingdom? Will self-determination be established for the entirety of Ireland with its future dependent on a majority vote of the island as whole, or will the principle of consent require a separate voice and vote just for the people of the six northern counties in determining the constitutional position of Northern Ireland? How does each party ground its opinion on the constitutional issues in its own appreciation of Northern Ireland's history and culture?

PREPARATION AND ASSIGNMENTS
Initial written essays presenting the context for the talks and the major issues to be discussed will sent by the chair(s) and the representatives of Britain and Ireland to the GM to be posted electronically before the session. All students should read core texts numbers 16 (Downing Street Declaration, 1993), 17 (Paramilitary Cease Fire Announcements, 1994), and 19 (the Mitchell Principles, 1996). The chair(s) and British and Irish representatives should also review core text number 18 (Ground Rules for Substantive All-Party Negotiations Issued by the British Government, 1996). What do the Unionists and Nationalists, respectively, support or condemn in the declaration overall? For your specific political views on decommissioning, review your role sheets and read the speeches appropriate for your position as a Unionist or Nationalist in sections E and F of the sources; particularly in core texts numbers 21 (Paisley), 22 (Ervine), 23 (Trimble), and 26 and 27 (Adams).

Cross-community parties should consult the Alliance Party's statement (no. 28).

Session 4. Second Meeting of the Multiparty Talks
AGENDA

Item B: Constitutional Issues (continued from previous meeting). Parties will continue to present their positions and attempt to come to a consensus on constitutional issues.

Item C: Strand 1, the Structure of Northern Ireland's Government. The parties should present their positions and proposals on relationships within Northern Ireland. If the constitutional debate leads toward a separate, devolved government for Northern Ireland, what institutions should be created to provide self-governance for the people there? What form should the executive and legislative powers take? How will fairness between the Unionist and Nationalist communities be guaranteed and cooperation encouraged? Should the governing system be based on a parliamentary system of majority rule or a form of power-sharing?

PREPARATION AND ASSIGNMENTS

Initial individual written essays from all the political party delegates will be sent to the GM and shared electronically before the session. Delegates should provide a reasoned argument for their views on the future settlement for Northern Ireland—these essays can discuss issues from any of the three strands that are vital to each party's objectives. In preparing these essays, all students should review their roles and the relevant statements and speeches in the core texts for a basic understanding of their sense of national identity (section B for Unionists and section C for Nationalists) and for their constitutional and political positions (section E for Unionists and section F for Nationalists). Cross-community parties (APNI and NIWC) should examine the ways in which the remarks of David Ervine (core text no. 22) and John Hume (no. 24), or the fact that each participant is a member of the European Union (no. 20), might suggest paths to achieve a settlement, along with reviewing the APNI statement (no. 28).

Session 5. Third Meeting of the Multiparty Talks
AGENDA

This session will begin with faction meetings where the parties can review their positions and develop strategies to reach out to possible allies. The chair will then reconvene the formal meeting.

Item C: Strand 1 (continued from previous meeting). The debate over the structure of Northern Ireland's government will continue. This session will add consideration of how the agreement can best restore respect in both communities for the police forces and judicial system in Northern Ireland. Does the nature of policing and justice need to be reformed? Should the members of the Unionist and Republican paramilitaries who are in prison continue their sentences as criminals or should they be released based on their claim to status as political prisoners? What rights need to be clearly stated? Can any structures be built to begin to cross community boundaries and integrate the state?

Item D: Agreement Options. At the end of the session, the chair will provide a draft outline of the options on the constitutional and strand issues that will need to be decided in the final agreement. They will also post the second essays written by the chair(s) and government representatives in which each highlights the choices that they believe are most important for achieving an agreement. After the session, all delegates should read through the draft outline and essays, consult with their own parties, and interact with the other parties that may be potential allies in order to determine which options they are willing to accept.

PREPARATION AND ASSIGNMENTS

All students should review the speeches in these core texts for basic disagreements over the organization of democracy in Northern Ireland, particularly numbers 21 (Paisley), 23 (Trimble) and 26 and 27 (Adams). In what ways do the remarks of David Ervine (core text no. 22), John Hume (no. 24), and the Alliance Party (no. 28) suggest alternatives that might provide a path toward a settlement? Students should also review their role sheets for their positions on policing and prisoners and relate those positions to the broader sense of nationalism espoused in the speeches and statements cited above.

Session 6. Fourth Meeting of the Multiparty Talks
AGENDA
Items D and E: Agreement Options and Strand 2.
Parties should present their positions and proposals on relationships within the island of Ireland in the context of an overall agreement. On what issues should there be consultation between the Republic of Ireland and the government of Northern Ireland? Will the Republic have any real authority over internal matters in the North? What will be the nature and status of any North-South institutions or councils? Will the determinations of those councils be merely consultative, needing the separate approval of the Northern Ireland Assembly, or will they have the direct authority to be implemented in Northern Ireland?

PREPARATION AND ASSIGNMENTS
In order to debate these issues, delegates should be aware of the positions that have been taken in the previous sessions, and the choices in drafts of options presented by the chair, as well as any progress they have made in negotiations with other groups. All delegates will write a second essay arguing for options or alternatives that they will support in a final agreement. These second essays should be sent to the GM and posted before the start of the meeting.

In preparing these second essays, delegates should concentrate on the issues that have created the most difficulty in trying to establish an agreement; reviewing again their roles and the context provided by the governments in core text number 16, the Downing Street Declaration of 1993. These essays should not just deal with technical details such as the makeup of the executive and the manner of voting but also present a coherent argument on the larger issues of national identity and democratic participation that have been raised by the discussions.

Session 7. Fifth Meeting of the Multiparty Talks
AGENDA
Item F: Presentation of a Final Agreement. The chair(s), in consultation with the British and Irish governments, will present a final proposal for the agreement (sent out electronically the day before the session). This final draft should be based on the input from the parties in the multiparty meetings and the written essays of the delegates.

The chair will lead the delegates through a combination of formal discussion and faction meetings as needed for any final negotiations or amendments. The parties to the talks will take up each strand in turn and debate the whole of the agreement. The parties will face a deadline of a final formal vote taking place fifteen minutes before the end of the session. *To pass, the agreement will need the votes of a majority of the parties in the talks as a whole as well as a majority of the individual representatives within each of the two communities—Unionist and Nationalist.*

PREPARATION AND ASSIGNMENTS
The chair(s), in consultation with the British and Irish governments, must prepare their final proposal for the agreement, based on input and essays from delegates, and send it to everyone the day before the session.

Referendum and Debriefing
Session 8. The Referendum
AGENDA
If the agreement was passed by the multiparty conference in the previous session, the GM will conduct a referendum in which the voters in Northern Ireland will cast a yes or no vote on the agreement.

PREPARATION AND ASSIGNMENTS
Each government representative and each political party will be responsible for presenting a brief argument for or against approval that is aimed at the larger public (delegates from smaller parties may join together in making this appeal; major parties may collaborate as well but must make sure that they

have materials that appeal to their own specific core voters). The parties should prepare materials—pamphlets, posters, brief campaign ads or videos, and the like—to appeal by words and symbolism to the general public. They should convey several specific reasons for casting a yes or no vote in the referendum. The presentations will be judged by the chair(s) and the GM for those most likely to resonate with voters. The most effective presentations may have an impact on the determination of the final popular vote.

Session 9. Debrief on the Talks and the Good Friday Agreement

The game master will lead the class in a discussion on the main themes and events of the game and compare them to the actual development of the multiparty talks. Students will discuss what happened in the game, reveal secrets, and talk about what happened in history, and how all of this relates to other themes in your course or to modern events.

4

Roles and Factions

The number of delegates for each party at the multiparty talks was determined by the percentage of votes they each received in the 1996 elections to the Northern Ireland Forum: UUP—24.2 percent; SDLP—21.4 percent; DUP—18.8 percent; Sinn Féin—15.5 percent; APNI—6.5 percent; UKUP—3.7 percent; PUP—3.5 percent; UDP—2.2 percent; NIWC—1 percent (note that the Labour Party also received 1 percent but is not represented in this game). All members of each party will receive the same victory objectives initially and should collaborate to achieve them. But individual members of the parties may have different tasks to perform or may be more or less open to compromise with other political parties.

Indeterminates: Political parties may be indeterminate on individual issues. Individual members of larger political parties may themselves be uncertain of their final votes as they struggle to reconcile their beliefs about the essence of the national community in Northern Ireland with the compromises on the table to end the Troubles. Students should be aware of the possibility of indeterminacy and look for representatives of other parties who may be open to alliances as they negotiate with other factions and attempt to build coalitions.

CHAIRS

Senator George Mitchell, chair: A former US senator, Mitchell came to Ireland in 1995 to develop economic initiatives as a special adviser to President Bill Clinton. He then served at the request of British prime minister John Major as chair with two colleagues, John de Chastelain and Harri Holkeri, of a special commission to make recommendations on decommissioning. In 1996 Major requested that Mitchell and his colleagues chair the multiparty talks. (Note that the roles of de Chastelain and Holkeri are only used in larger classes. When they are in the game, Mitchell chairs the day-to-day meetings of the talks, de Chastelain works with the factions on the decommissioning issue, and Holkeri works with the factions to understand possible power-sharing and consociational structures.)

John de Chastelain, cochair: A well-respected Canadian general who served twice as chief of the Canadian Defence Staff (1989–93 and 1994–95), was Canada's ambassador to the United States in 1993–94, and commanded Canada's peacekeeping troops in Somalia in the early 1990s. Before the multiparty talks, he served on the International Body on Arms with Mitchell and Holkeri.

Harri Holkeri, cochair: A well-respected former prime minister of Finland from 1987 to 1991 and member of the board of directors of the Bank of Finland until 1997. Before the multiparty talks he served with Mitchell and de Chastelain on the International Body on Arms.

GOVERNMENT REPRESENTATIVES

Great Britain government representative: This is a direct aide to the British secretary for Northern Ireland, Mo Mowlam, who, with the new Labour prime minister Tony Blair, will be very involved in guiding the British position at the talks. It is possible that the new Labour government is more open to creative solutions to the Troubles than the previous government of John Major, which was dependent on Unionist votes in Parliament.

Republic of Ireland government representative: This is a top aide to the taoiseach (the equivalent of a British prime minister) Bertie Ahern. Ahern's party, Fianna Fáil, has its roots in the Republicans who fought the partition of Ireland in the 1920s, both against Britain and then in a civil war with the Irish Free State. The party was created by Eamon de Valera in 1926 to give this faction a legal voice again in Irish politics after it lost the civil war. In recent years Fianna Fáil has been open to negotiations with Great Britain. Former taoiseach Albert Reynolds jointly issued the Downing Street Declaration in 1993 with then British prime minister John Major. Ahern, like British prime minister Tony Blair, will be closely involved in the multiparty talks.

Unionists

Ulster Unionist Party (UUP): The largest of the Unionist parties in Northern Ireland, with close links to the Protestant Orange Order. The UUP governed Northern Ireland from 1921 to 1972, participated in the Sunningdale Agreement of 1973–74, and opposed the Anglo-Irish Agreement of 1985. It did not publicly oppose the Downing Street Declaration of 1993 but entered the multiparty talks at Stormont concerned about major issues such as preserving majority rule and demanding full decommissioning. Its party leader is David Trimble.

Democratic Unionist Party (DUP): The second-largest of the Unionist parties was formed in 1971 by Ian Paisley and Desmond Boal and led by Paisley. It was firmly opposed to the Sunningdale and Anglo-Irish Agreements as well as the Downing Street

Declaration, vigorously protects the Protestant faith, and opposes any negotiations that threaten the position of Northern Ireland within the United Kingdom.

Progressive Unionist Party (PUP): A small Unionist party that is closely linked to the Ulster Volunteer Force (UVF), a Loyalist paramilitary group that counts Gusty Spence as one of its leaders. Although the party was formed in 1979, it became more prominent when it was seen as the political voice of the UVF after that group declared a ceasefire in 1994. It is led by Hugh Smyth and David Ervine. It is determined to keep Northern Ireland in the United Kingdom, but as a working-class party it realizes that Protestants and Catholics face a stagnant economy because the Troubles have stunted growth. Thus, it is more flexible in looking for solutions and willing to sit down and talk with the Nationalists.

United Kingdom Unionist Party (UKUP): A small Unionist party formed and led by Robert McCartney in 1995 after he broke from the UUP. The UKUP campaigned for Northern Ireland to become more closely integrated with the United Kingdom.

Ulster Democratic Party (UDP): This small Unionist party was formed in 1989 and led by Gary McMichael, John White, and David Adams. It was closely linked to the Ulster Defence Association, a Loyalist paramilitary group that carried out many of its violent activities under the label of the Ulster Freedom Fighters (UFF). It believed its tactics helped force the IRA/Sinn Féin to the negotiating table. It has little tolerance for political leaders, such as Ian Paisley, who use inflammatory language but have not risked their own lives as soldiers. The UDP is open to negotiations with Catholics and power-sharing if that can lead to an end to the Troubles, a devolved government, and a more prosperous economy in Northern Ireland.

Nationalists

Social Democratic and Labour Party (SDLP): The largest Nationalist party in Northern Ireland. It was founded in 1970 and initially led by Gerald Fitt; John Hume became leader of the party in 1979. The party supported civil rights campaigns in the 1970s and opposed violence, preferring to work for constitutional solutions. While still believing in the ultimate goal of national unification, it placed priority on winning rights and improving living conditions in Northern Ireland itself and was willing to take part in the power-sharing executive established briefly by the Sunningdale Agreement in 1974. It supported the Downing Street Declaration of 1993.

Sinn Féin: The second-largest Nationalist party, representing many of the Republicans who were dedicated to the realization of a united Ireland. Sinn Féin supported the Irish Republican Army (IRA) and is viewed by many Unionists as the political wing of the IRA. Although it claims historic ties back to the original Sinn Féin party formed in 1906, its modern version was formed in 1970 after a split between the Marxist Official IRA and the Provisional IRA (also known as the Provos; when we refer to the IRA in this game it is to the Provisional IRA). Originally believing in abstentionism, it began to take part in elections using the popularity of the hunger strikers in 1981. It is the only party to run candidates both in Northern Ireland and in the Republic of Ireland. Led by Gerry Adams and Martin McGuiness, Sinn Féin was barred from the multiparty talks when the IRA ended its ceasefire in 1996 and began a new bombing campaign.

Cross-Community Parties

Alliance Party of Northern Ireland (APNI): The small Alliance Party was formed in 1970 and while supporting union with Great Britain has tried to develop cross-community support and is open to developing formal links with the Republic of Ireland. It is led by John Alderdice.

Northern Ireland Women's Coalition (NIWC): The NIWC was formed in 1996 as a cross-community party to offer an alternative to the sectarian groups. It advocated reconciliation through dialogue and also sought to promote the participation of women in politics. It was led by Monica McWilliams, Pearl Sagar, and Janice Morrice.

5
Core Texts

In order to play the game successfully, one must have a basic grasp on the following documents. Critical passages have been italicized to assist your comprehension. The original English spelling has been maintained in all documents.

SECTION A. DEFENDING CULTURAL COMMUNITIES: PERSONAL MOTIVES FOR SECTARIAN AND POLITICAL WAR

The Troubles in Northern Ireland are deeply rooted in the history of conflict and rebellion that is detailed in the "Historical Background" chapter. But the initial motivation for many of the members of the Loyalist and Republican paramilitaries was a simple desire to defend their own sectarian community from the British or from members of the other religious group. These excerpts from interviews with participants will help you to understand the fears, hatred, desire for revenge, and willingness to sacrifice for the defense of their own community that motivated many of the soldiers in the conflict. Combine these emotions with the philosophical and political explanations of the conflict that you will find in the Unionist and Nationalist documents provided later in the core texts.

1. "Bernadette Devlin on Loyalist Ambush at Burntollet," 1969

Political activist and Nationalist member of Parliament (MP) Bernadette Devlin participated in a civil rights march that was ambushed by Loyalists at Burntollet on New Year's Day 1969.

Source: "Bernadette Devlin on Loyalist Ambush at Burntollet," Alpha History, accessed 1 July 2019, https://alphahistory.com/northernireland/bernadette-devlin-burntollet-ambush-1969/.

And then we came to Burntollet Bridge, and from lanes at each side of the road a curtain of bricks and boulders and bottles brought the march to a halt. From the lanes burst hordes of screaming people wielding planks of wood, bottles, laths, iron bars, crowbars, cudgels studded with nails, and they waded into the march beating the hell out of everybody.

I was a very clever girl; cowardice makes you clever. Before this onslaught, our heads-down, arms-linked tactics were no use whatever, and people began to panic and run. Immediately my mind went back to Derry on October 5th and I remembered the uselessness of running. As I stood there I could see a great big lump of flatwood, like a plank out of an orange-box, getting nearer and nearer my face, and there were two great nails sticking out of it. By a quick reflex action, my hand reached my face before the wood did, and immediate two nails went into the back of my hand. Just after that I was struck on the back of the knees with this bit of wood which had failed to get me in the face and fell to the ground.

And then my brain began to tick. "Now, Bernadette," I said, "what is the best thing to do? If you leave your arms and legs out, they'll be broken. You can have your skull cracked or your face destroyed." So I rolled up in a ball on the road, tucked my knees in, tucked my elbows in, and covered my face with one hand and the crown of my head with the other. Through my fingers, I could see legs standing round me: about six people were busily involved in trying to beat me into the ground, and I could feel dull thuds landing on my back and head. Finally, these men muttered something incoherent about leaving that one, and tore off across the fields after somebody else.

When everything was quiet, and five seconds had gone by without my feeling anything, I decided it was time to take my head up. I had a wee peer round, ducked again as a passing Paisleyite threw a swipe at me, and then got up. *What had been a march was a shambles.* The first few rows had managed to put a spurt on when the attack came, had got through the ambush and were safely up the road. The rest of us were all over the place. *The attackers were beating marchers into the ditches, and across the ditches into the river.* People were being dragged half-conscious out of the river. Others were being pursued across the fields into the woods. Others had been trapped on the road and were being given a good hiding where they stood.

As I got shakily to my feet and looked round, I saw a young fellow getting a thrashing from four or five Paisleyites with a policeman looking on: the policeman was pushing the walking-wounded marchers up the road to join the front rows and doing nothing to prevent the attack. "What the bloody hell d'you think you're doing?" I shouted at him, hereupon he gave me a vigorous shove and said. "Get up the road to the rest of your mates, stupid bitch." (Policemen always call me a stupid bitch, and I deny that I'm stupid.) . . . Even the other policeman protested to the fellow who had pushed me. "Mind the way you throw those kids about they're getting enough."

2. Motivation for Joining the IRA: Excerpts from Kevin Toolis's *Rebel Hearts*

In August 1969, the attacks on the civil rights marchers turned into violent confrontations between Catholics and the Royal Ulster Constabulary in Derry/Londonderry's Battle of the Bogside and then sectarian rioting in Belfast that led to 1,800 families being burned out of their homes, 1,500 of them Catholic. In Rebel Hearts, Kevin Toolis tells the story of the Finucane brothers, three of whom joined the IRA and one, Patrick, who was murdered after serving as a defense attorney for IRA members. Seamus Finucane, whose interview is excerpted below, watched Catholic homes being torched on Perry Street in Belfast in 1969 and then saw the Protestants seize his own family's home and possessions. He soon joined the Provisional IRA.

Source: Kevin Toolis, *Rebel Hearts: Journeys within the IRA's Soul* (London: Picador, 1995), 104–5, 114.

Percy Street was a turning point; it was our introduction into politics. We lived through fifty years of misrule by Stormont, all the bigotry, the gerrymandering and sectarian killings. I can remember my brother John going for jobs and once they heard where you lived or what school you were at, then they knew you were a Catholic: "Ah don't call us, we'll call you." We were always at the tail end of things. But after 1969 it was like: "Out of the ashes arose the Provisionals" and "The great only appear great because we are on our knees." *There was a sense that this was the time to change things and stop being pushed around, stop being downtrodden.* "Let's get off our knees and do something—start fighting back." None of us were brought into the world to become involved in politics and fight wars. The politics of the struggle ended up taking over our lives.

[Seamus's brother John was killed while on active duty for the IRA. Another brother, Martin, admired John's choice to defend his community:]

I was very proud of my brother because he had given up so much of his life not only to protect me but to protect his community. He spent many nights patrolling the estate with a rifle in case anything happened say from a Loyalist attack. He manned checkpoints and foot patrols in his own community and I respected that. He was defending the community against the British Army. I still reflect even now on the few weeks I did have with him, the last talk, the last smile. I still try and keep that image of his face within my memory.

[Another brother, Dermot, was impressed by John's funeral:]

The local IRA companies openly marched down the street, sixty men all in formation, and they were called in Irish to stop outside our door and then in single file they marched in to pay their respects. It was very military looking and organized. My older brothers told me that it was the biggest funeral up until that time to leave Andersonstown. *I remember being very proud that John was getting a military funeral.* I remember people on the sidelines were giving the coffin a military salute; I was told that a few British soldiers saluted it as a mark of respect. The crowds were massive. Some people went there because he was an IRA man, others because they knew our family and we were a respectable family, and others came because at that time in the IRA you had ranks and officers and our John was a lieutenant.

[According to Toolis,] John's death on active service only intensified the family's commitment to the IRA.

3. Motivation for Loyalist Violence: Excerpts from Peter Taylor's *Loyalists*

Journalist Peter Taylor interviewed Loyalist paramilitaries who were frank about being willing to kill Catholics in retaliation for Protestant deaths. For example, he talked with Eddie Kinner, one of three members of the Ulster Volunteer Force (UVF) who set a bomb at a Catholic bar in Belfast in March 1975.

Source: Peter Taylor, *Loyalists: War and Peace in Northern Ireland* (New York: TV Books, 1999), 144.

They had been told that an IRA meeting was taking place inside [a bar they were ordered to bomb by the UVF] and never thought to question the intelligence. "As far as I was concerned," Kinner told me, "the UVF had come back with that information and they had selected the target so I was prepared to go and attack it." I asked him if he was really concerned about the precise nature of the target.

[INTERVIEWER (I):] Did you care if it wasn't a meeting of republicans and it just a Catholic bar?
[KINNER (K):] I didn't particularly care.
[I:] If it was a Catholic target.
[K:] Yes.
[I:] A sectarian target.
[K:] Yes.
[I:] That's the way you were thinking at that time?
[K:] My attitude was that they are inflicting that on my community. They [Catholics] harbour IRA men that were carrying that out in my community. They didn't expel IRA men from their community that attacked my community.
[I:] But it really wasn't like that. The vast majority of Catholics didn't support the IRA. People in that bar didn't necessarily support the IRA. They were just innocent Catholics having a drink.
[K:] I think, in terms of how I felt then, it didn't matter.

4. Bobby Sands, "The Harvest Britain Has Sown"

Bobby Sands, who had joined the IRA after his family had been forced out of their home in Belfast, was imprisoned for a second time on weapons charges in 1977. He joined the blanket protest against "criminal status" and then became the IRA's leader in the prison. (Both the Republican and Loyalist prisoners founded paramilitary structures in the prisons and used them to educate and train their members.) Sands went on hunger strike on 1 March 1981 and after sixty-six days became the first of ten IRA hunger strikers to die, after winning election as an MP to the British Parliament. He secretly wrote memoirs while in prison. In this excerpt he indicates both the sense of sacrifice that underlay the Republican movement and the continuing hatred that British policies engendered.

Source: Bobby Sands, *Writings from Prison* (1983; Boulder, CO: Roberts Rinehart, 1997), 94–95.

A stretch of tarmac surrounded by barbed wire and steel is the only view from my cell window. I'm told it's an exercise yard. I wouldn't know. In my fourteen months in H Block, I haven't been allowed to walk in the fresh air. I am on "cellular confinement" today. That is the three days out of every fourteen when my only possessions, three blankets and a mattress, are removed, leaving a blanket and a chamber pot.

I'm left to pass the day like this, from 7.30 a.m. to 8.30 p.m. How I spend my day is determined by the weather. If it's reasonably warm, it's possible to sit on the floor, stare at the white walls, and pass a few hours day-dreaming. But otherwise I must spend my day continuously pacing the cell to prevent the cold chilling through to my bones. Even after my bedding is returned at 8.30 p.m. hours will pass before the circulation returns to my feet and legs. . . .

To accept the status of criminal would be to degrade myself and to admit that the cause that I believe in and cherish is wrong. When thinking of the men and women who sacrificed life itself, my suffering seems insignificant. There have been many attempts to break my will but each one has made me even more determined....

I see it also in the faces of my comrades at Mass: *the hatred in their eyes.* One day these young men will be fathers and these attitudes will inevitably be passed on to their children.

This is the harvest Britain has sown: her actions will eventually seal the fate of her rule in Ireland....

They may hold our bodies in the most inhuman conditions, but, while our minds remain free, our victory is assured!

5. The Day-to-Day Sectarian Tension of the Troubles: Excerpts from Kevin Toolis's *Rebel Hearts*

While the "Historical Background" chapter focuses on the events in major cities, this excerpt from Rebel Hearts indicates the day-to-day tension experienced even in smaller communities. The IRA blamed the British for the oppression of the Nationalist community in Northern Ireland and saw as legitimate targets not only British soldiers but any person who gave support to the British presence or to the Royal Ulster Constabulary (RUC). But as is noted here, since most of these targets were also Protestant, it was difficult for the Unionist community to tell the difference between political and sectarian motivations for violence. This excerpt discusses the atmosphere in a small community following the IRA murder of a council worker (Private Gibson) who was also a part-time member of the Ulster Defence Regiment (UDR), which served as a support unit for the RUC; and the fear of a Sinn Féin councillor about a tit-for-tat reaction from the Loyalists.

Source: Kevin Toolis, *Rebel Hearts: Journeys within the IRA's Soul* (London: Picador, 1995), 59.

In a bid to shield him from the IRA, Private Gibson's employers, Cookstown District Council, had frequently switched him between jobs. On the morning of his murder Gibson, who had been in the UDR for less than a month, was only assigned to that particular bin lorry minutes before it left the depot, yet the IRA were waiting. Their intelligence was remarkable; someone, probably several people, had built up a superb little dossier on Private Gibson. In a place like Tyrone, where each community had to cross through the enemy's territory on a daily basis, and every hedgerow had eyes and ears, it did not take long to find out enough to kill a man. Private Gibson must have been spotted in his UDR uniform, either on patrol or at home in Coagh; someone else must have identified him as a council worker; the bin lorry route would have been checked; enough information, from outwardly ordinary members of the nationalist community, would have been collated to arrange the hit; the IRA leadership sent their gunmen in to stiff Ned.

The IRA did not fight a sectarian war. It did not, as Francie McNally pointed out, kill Ned Gibson just because he was a Protestant; they killed him because he was a member of the UDR. But since every member of the UDR was a Protestant, the distinction was understandably lost on their relatives and friends. To these people, Ned was not an anonymous statistic digit in some endless struggle; Ned was part of their small community, a brother, a nephew, a colleague and a comrade in their war against the IRA. It was inevitable that Tyrone's Protestant community saw the IRA campaign as sectarian warfare against them. In revenge for Gibson's killing a Protestant mob in Coagh attacked the homes of the remaining few Catholic families in the village, later forcing them to abandon their houses. It would have been foolish to believe that Loyalist paramilitaries in Tyrone needed much of an excuse to kill Republicans, but after Ned Gibson's killing it was clear thar some of them positively decided to strike back. A UVF death squad was formed.

Francie McNally, already the focus of Protestant rage as the sole Sinn Féin councillor in the Coagh area, went straight to the top of the UVF target list. "After Gibson was shot, whenever I was stopped by the UDR on the road they started to call me Ned, because I was a Cookstown District councillor and the intelligence on Gibson was fucking top-class.

They thought I was the only one that had that intelligence available to me. They haven't changed their mind about that yet."

Death threats forced Francie McNally to abandon his isolated bungalow home in favour of a barricaded council house in the middle of an Ardboe housing estate [a Catholic area]. Standing in his kitchen, he pointed out through the window, past the twelve-foot-high sharpened metal stakes that surrounded his back garden. *"Do you see that house, two hundred yards away? That is where it begins—that is hostile territory. Those people want to kill me. I suppose they really do hate me."* And then, incongruously, he burst out laughing.

SECTION B. COMPETING CONCEPTS OF NATIONALISM: UNIONISM AND LOYALISM

6. The Ulster Covenant, 1912

The Ulster Covenant (fully titled the Ulster Solemn League and Covenant) was drafted in September 1912 by Edward Carson and James Craig in opposition to the British Parliament's third Home Rule bill, legislation that would establish a self-governing parliament in Ireland. The Ulster Covenant was signed by almost 250,000 men; a similar declaration was signed by 230,000 women.

Source: "Ulster Covenant," Alpha History, accessed 1 July 2019, https://alphahistory.com/northernirlenad/ulster-covenent-1912.

Being convinced in our consciences that Home Rule would be disastrous to the material well-being of Ulster as well as of the whole of Ireland, subversive of our civil and religious freedom, destructive of our citizenship, and perilous to the unity of the Empire, we, whose names are underwritten, men of Ulster, loyal subjects of His Gracious Majesty King George V, humbly relying on the God whom our fathers in days of stress and trial confidently trusted, do hereby pledge ourselves in solemn Covenant, throughout this our time of threatened calamity, to stand by one another in defending, for ourselves and our children, our cherished position of equal citizenship in the United Kingdom, and in using all means which may be found necessary to defeat the present conspiracy to set up a Home Rule Parliament in Ireland. And in the event of such a Parliament being forced upon us, we further solemnly and mutually pledge ourselves to refuse to recognise its authority.

In sure confidence that God will defend the right, we hereto subscribe our names.

7. James Craig, Parliamentary Speech: "A Protestant Government for Protestant People," 21 November 1934

Craig was the Unionist prime minister of Northern Ireland from 1921 to 1940.

Source: "Quotations on the Topic of Discrimination," CAIN, accessed 1 July 2019, https://cain.ulster.ac.uk/issues/discrimination/quotes.

THE PRIME MINISTER [Sir James Craig]: The hon. Member says that all our appointments are carried out on a religious basis. I would like to go into this somewhat fully. The appointments made by the Government are made as far as we can possibly manage it of loyal men and women. Why not? And what objection can there possibly be to those who are upholding Ulster as part of the great British Empire and the United Kingdom, seeing that we have not got saturated through the place those who acquiesce in the policy of the hon. Members opposite, of endeavouring to break down the machinery of government given to us by the British people? Surely nothing could be clearer than that. If a man is a Roman Catholic, if he is fitted for the job, provided he is loyal to the core, he has as good a chance of appointment as anybody else; and if a Protestant is not loyal to the core he has no more chance than a similar Roman Catholic.

MR. O'NEILL: How do you test their loyalty?

THE PRIME MINISTER: There are ways of finding that out. The hon. Member knows just as well as I do there are ways of discovering whether a man is heart and soul in carrying out the intention of the Act of 1920, which was given to the Ulster people in order to save them from being swallowed up in a Dublin Parliament. *Therefore, it is undoubtedly our duty and our privilege, and always will be, to see that those appointed by us possess the most unimpeachable loyalty to the King and Constitution. That is my whole object in carrying on a Protestant Government for a Protestant people.* I repeat it in this House.

8. Letter from the Orange Order to the Catholic Residents of the Garvaghy Road, 4 June 1997

The Orange Order was formed in 1795 to defend Loyalism and Protestantism. It carried out numerous parades each year to promote Unionism and honor the past victories over Catholic rebels, particularly that of King William of Orange over the Catholic King James II at the Battle of the Boyne in 1690. The following letter is an attempt by one Orange Order chapter to explain the significance of the parades for the Unionist community and to urge Catholic residents to respect their order of march. This letter was delivered on 4 June 1997.

Source: "Parades," CAIN, accessed 4 May 2019, https://cain.ulster.ac.uk/issues/parade/docs/00040697.

Dear Resident,

We are writing to all the residents of the Garvaghy Road area to explain our position about the annual walk by members of Portadown District Orangemen from the service of worship at Drumcree parish church in July.

This is a sincere and genuine attempt to deal with the many misconceptions concerning the walk and there are a number of points we would like to make for your information:

1. *The service on the first Sunday in July is partly to remember those who died at the Battle of the Somme in 1916.* We pay tribute to all those of both communities who died for the cause of peace and justice.
2. The Orange Order is traditionally a parading organisation. *We see our parade as an outward witness to our sincere belief in the Reformed Faith.* For that reason, we see attacks on our parades as both a denial of civil liberties and an attack on our religion. For us, this is as distressing as the disgraceful protest—which we unreservedly condemn—outside Harryville chapel.

3. In the interests of harmony, mutual respect and reconciliation the Orange Order has acknowledged objections raised by the nationalist community and has already implemented the following principles for the Drumcree Church parade:
   a. The number of parades in the area has been reduced from ten to one in the past ten years.
   b. Only members of Portadown District parade.
   c. No bands take part which could be perceived as antagonistic to our nationalist neighbours. Accordion bands lead the parade playing hymn music that is common to both traditions.
   d. The Orangemen walk four abreast so that the walk will pass in any one given point in less than five minutes.
   e. The Order marshals and disciplines its own members to ensure there will be no confrontation on our part. If this was reciprocated, then there would only be a need for a minimal police presence.
   f. The right to walk peacefully and in a dignified manner and the right to protest in a peaceful and dignified manner should not be denied to anyone.

It is the sincere hope of the Orange Order that the vast majority of the people of Portadown will work together in a new spirit of tolerance to defeat extremists who want confrontation this summer.

As a matter of principle, we cannot be involved in talks with convicted terrorists because of what they have inflicted on our community. But we do want to listen to all those within the community who want to promote harmony and mutual respect among the people of Portadown and would welcome constructive comments which should be sent to the following address:

Co Armagh Grand Orange Lodge, c/o House of Orange, 65 Dublin Road, Belfast BT2 7HE.

We sincerely hope that this letter will go some way towards building up intercommunity confidence and respect so that we can look forward not only to a peaceful summer but to a more peaceful and tolerant era for all the people of our land.

Yours faithfully,
Denis J Watson, William T Bingham, County Grand Master, County Grand Chaplain.

9. Progressive Unionist Party: Excerpts from "The Principles of Loyalism"

This statement initially developed in the 1990s to help lay the rational foundation for Unionism. This version was posted on the party's website in 2002 but reflects the arguments put forward at the time of the negotiations.

Source: "Principles of Loyalism: An Internal Discussion Paper," Progressive Unionist Party, accessed 23 April 2019, http://pupni.com/assets/images/articles/Principles_of_Loyalism.pdf.

The Principles of Loyalism is an attempt to put forward the key elements of the loyalist cause that were established by the founding fathers of unionism at the time of the Home Rule crisis. Loyalists need a set of core principles based on those principles that enjoyed the popular support of the unionist community in the struggle against Home Rule. Such a set of principles is clearly set out in Ulster's Solemn League and Covenant and this is an appropriate starting point for any serious discussion on the subject. This historic document, which was endorsed by some 450,000 Ulster men and women from all sections of the pro-unionist community, has been said by some to be the Birth Certificate of modern Ulster. It is certainly the one document that summarises why Ulster Unionists in 1912 sought to ensure that Northern Ireland remained an integral part of the United Kingdom. That Northern Ireland remained within the United Kingdom when the rest of Ireland seceded from the union is due to both the political resolve and the military resolve of those who signed the Covenant and backed up their intentions with the formation of a volunteer army.

The Solemn League and Covenant was to the birth of Northern Ireland what the Revolutionary Settlement of 1689 was to the birth of Britain's Constitutional Monarchy and the principle of parliamentary sovereignty. It was, and remains, a revolutionary document insofar as it claimed that the will of the British citizens of Northern Ireland took precedence over the will of the Imperial Parliament. It established a covenantal relationship between the British citizens of Northern Ireland which, in the absence of it being rescinded by the people of Northern Ireland, remains the foundation document of Loyalism.

Today's loyalists are the covenant children of those who signed the Covenant and as such have a duty to maintain those core principles of that Covenant which remain appropriate in the 21st century. These include: 1. The Material well-being of Ulster; 2. Civil and Religious Freedom; 3. Equal Citizenship within the United Kingdom and 4. The Use of Armed Resistance. Each of these core principles ought to provide a basis for unity within unionism and, in particular, within the loyalist paramilitary-linked constituencies. . . .

A loyalism that is based on the core principles of the Solemn League & Covenant has more to offer the people of Ulster than violence. A philosophy that is based simply on violence will lock our people and our communities into a perpetual cycle of alienation, conflict and violence. It also misrepresents what loyalism is really about.

A loyalism that is based on the principles of the Solemn League and Covenant is a loyalism that is committed to seeking the material (social & economic) well being of the people of Northern Ireland. It is a loyalism that is genuinely committed to upholding the principles of civil and religious liberty for all citizens of Northern Ireland. It is a loyalism that is committed to defending for ourselves and our children the principles of equal citizenship; and it is a loyalism that is proud to identify with peoples of the Commonwealth and with the values, principles and priorities of the Commonwealth. Yes, there is a place for armed resistance to unjust political impositions and to terror campaigns, but a principled loyalism that has its roots in the Solemn League & Covenant has much more to offer the people of Ulster.

Principle 1: The framers of the Solemn League and Covenant had a concern, not just for the constitutional issues and the principles of civil and religious liberty, but also for the material well being of the people.

Principle 2: The framers of the Solemn League and Covenant believed that an Irish Home Rule Parliament, comprised in the main of Catholic Nationalists who were committed to a Confessional State, would be "subversive of our civil and religious freedom" and could never afford them the freedoms that were essential to the development of a just and equitable society. Even the most casual reading of Irish history will find the issue of civil and religious freedom a cause for concern for Ulster Protestants. Civil and religious freedom is essential to the development of a just, equitable and pluralist society.

Religious liberty can flourish only if the State leaves religion alone. Citizens must be free to practice religion or not to practice religion without government interference . . . in the course of time the principle of civil and religious freedom has become an integral part of the British way of life.

The policies of both the Free State Government under Cosgrove and the Irish Republic under Eamon de Valera proved that the fears of Ulster Unionists were well founded. Until recently the cry "Home Rule is Rome Rule" was a fair reflection of the confessional nature of both the Irish Constitution and Irish Politics. In recent years the Irish Republic has become more liberal and pluralist, but it remains our belief that *the United Kingdom is better suited to the development of a multi-faith pluralist society than the Irish Republic. Indeed, it may be argued that the republican concept of citizenship is inimical to pluralism.* . . .

The papal "Ne Temere" decree announced by the Vatican in 1907 was rigidly enforced under both the Free State and the Irish Republic. This decree forced Protestant partners in a mixed marriage to formally sign a document stating that all children of the marriage would be raised in the Catholic Faith and was largely responsible for the marked decline in the

Protestant population from approximately 11 percent at the time of the secession to approximately 3 percent today.

In an attempt to keep the new Irish state free from anti-Catholic influences the Free State Government established a board of Censors under the 1929 Censorship Act. While this Act obviously affected the importation and distribution of Protestant and socialist literature it also affected many Irish writers. Some of Ireland's best writers—Clarke, Shaw, Gogarty, O'Flaherty, Moore, Hackett—fell foul of the censors. . . .

The Irish Republic under de Valera committed itself to the development of a society that reinforced its Catholicism. As early as 1931 de Valera claimed "there was an Irish solution that had no reference to any other country; a solution that came from our traditional attitude to life that was Irish and Catholic. That was the solution they were going to stand for so long as they were Catholic." Four years later, in his St. Patrick's Day address to the nation, de Valera made it quite clear that Ireland was a Catholic nation —"Since the coming of St Patrick 1500 years ago Ireland has been a Christian and a Catholic nation" and, he concluded, "she will remain a Catholic nation."

There was no mistaking where de Valera stood—Ireland was, and would continue to be, a Catholic nation. Nationalists are quick to point out that Sir James Craig, when prime minister of Northern Ireland, referred to Northern Ireland as a "Protestant state for a Protestant people." The wording attributed to Craig is incorrect and what he did say is never set in context. Craig's words, which were spoken in 1934 (three years after de Valera's), were "in the South they boasted of a Catholic state. They still boast of Southern Ireland being a Catholic state. All I boast of is that we are a Protestant Parliament and a Protestant state." De Valera's attitude provides no moral justification for Craig's position, but it does put it in context. . . .

There are indications that Sinn Féin, in spite of its public commitment to non-sectarian politics, is at heart a Catholic Nationalist party. Sinn Féin spokespersons repeatedly refer to the Irish community indiscriminately as "the Catholic community," "the Nationalist community" and "the Republican Community," thus reminding Protestants that even as we move into the 21st century the Republican Movement sees itself primarily as a Catholic Nationalist movement which holds the title deeds to the term "Irish." . . .

A loyalist response to the development of a Catholic Confessional State should not be the establishment of a Protestant Confessional State. If equal citizenship within the United Kingdom is to have any real meaning for loyalists, we must seek to develop a multi-cultural and multi-faith society that is in keeping with the rest of the United Kingdom.

Nationalists will complain that we are harping back to the old days. That we have too long a memory and need to draw a line under the past and concentrate on the present and the future. At the same time they are quite happy to harp back to the penal laws, the famine and allegations of discrimination under the old Stormont regime. Nationalism demands the right to embrace the politics of victim-hood while denying that right to unionists.

In highlighting the fact that the fears of our forbears regarding the threat to civil and religious liberty under a Home Rule Parliament were grounded in reality we do not ignore the fact that the Catholic minority in Northern Ireland suffered under a Protestant-Unionist dominated Stormont Government. De Valera's Catholic Constitution for a Catholic Nation was mirrored in Unionism's A Protestant Parliament for a Protestant People. The infringement of civil and religious liberty in one political jurisdiction does not make it right to replicate those infringements in another jurisdiction. . . .

We must acknowledge that civil and religious liberty is a basic human right that must be afforded to all people. . . .

We believe that the multi-cultural multi-faith pluralist society that is being developed across the United Kingdom provides the basis for such freedoms.

Principle 3: *Our forbears believed that Ulster's incorporation into an independent Irish State would* *be destructive of (their) citizenship* and pledged to stand by one another in "defending for ourselves and our children our cherished position of equal citizenship in the United Kingdom."

Citizenship within the context of the United Kingdom is about political identity rather than about national identity. Those citizens of the United Kingdom who regard themselves as Scottish, English, Welsh or Irish in terms of national identity are still able to enjoy full citizenship within the United Kingdom. The majority of Scotsmen and women see no contradiction in being Scottish and British. In the United States we regularly hear of people identifying themselves as Irish Americans. Why then should there be a contradiction in being both Irish and British? . . .

In the choice between citizenship within a broader pluralist United Kingdom that is inclusive of all the peoples of these islands and that draws upon the culture and traditions of the several historic kingdoms and provinces as well as the culture and traditions of ethnic communities, and citizenship within a more narrow and exclusive geographical union that is exclusive in terms of culture, religion and national identity the unionist community has consistently chosen the former. . . .

The peoples who form the unionist community come from a number of diverse cultures and traditions—Irish, Scottish, English, Welsh and some of Huguenot descent. Thus they wish to maintain citizenship within a state that acknowledges and validates their historic family origins and the traditions and culture that flow from those historic roots. *Citizenship for the British subject is not about a national identity or cultural exclusiveness. It is about sharing a political identity than transcends religion, culture, language and ethnicity. In short, it is about living in a multi-cultural and multi-ethnic pluralist society rather than in a society where citizenship is based on national identity, religion and cultural exclusiveness.*

As the Liberal Unionist, Arthur Aughey, has rightly noted, "The idea of the Union is the willing community of citizens united not by creed, colour or ethnicity but by a recognition of the authority of the Union."

The United Kingdom is thus able to facilitate pluralism whereas the Irish Republic, which links citizenship to a single national identity, is inimical to pluralism.

Our forbears believed, and we share those beliefs, that the incorporation of Northern Ireland into an independent all-Ireland republic would be destructive both of their British citizenship and of their very concept of citizenship. The distinctive anti-British ethos of Irish Nationalism convinced our forbears that an independent Irish Parliament would undermine and ultimately destroy their culture and traditions. They believed that it was only by maintaining inviolate their citizenship within the United Kingdom that their sense of Britishness could be maintained. The unionist community in Northern Ireland is not alone in wishing to maintain their British connection. Some 30 percent of the world's population in fifty-four free and independent countries, including thirty-three republics, choose to belong to the Commonwealth of Nations. Why? Because of their shared history with the United Kingdom. . . .

While the framers of the Solemn League & Covenant professed loyalty to the Crown they made it clear that their first loyalty was to wishes of the people of Ulster. Since the Crown, in a Constitutional Monarchy, is subject to the will of Parliament our loyalty to the Crown was and remains conditional upon Parliament's recognition of the expressed will of the people of Northern Ireland. *Thus our loyalty to the Crown is conditional upon Parliament endorsing and protecting the wishes of the people of Northern Ireland to maintain inviolate their British citizenship.*

There is a reciprocal loyalty. The loyalist community will honour its obligations and fulfil its duties to Parliament so long as Parliament acknowledges and upholds our right to equal citizenship within the United Kingdom. As citizens of the United Kingdom we expect to be given the same rights as those enjoyed by citizens in Scotland, England and Wales, and one of the most basic of those rights is the right to have our citizenship endorsed, validated and defended.

Our citizenship is not at the disposal of any particular British Parliament or Monarch but belongs to the citizens themselves. No Parliament or Monarch has the legal or moral authority to expel the unionist community from the Union or to impose upon it conditions of citizenship that are not applicable to citizens in Scotland, England or Wales. Thus *any attempt to impose joint sovereignty or any other measure that would diminish our British citizenship will be resisted.*

Principle 4: The Use of Armed Resistance

Thus, by the end of 1912 a force of some 90,000 volunteers was being prepared to resist the imposition of Home Rule should the Imperial Parliament so decree.

The Ulster Unionist Council was quite prepared to set aside the Rule of Law in order to defend the right of the Ulster people to resist unjust political impositions. The covenanters also stated "in the event of such a parliament being forced upon us we further solemnly and mutually pledge ourselves to refuse to recognise its authority." Resistance to the imposition of Home Rule would be through both armed resistance and civil disobedience. It is clear that the Ulster Unionist Council and the 450,000 people who signed the Covenant believed that the will of the people must be exercised, if necessary, outside the Rule of Law. . . .

The fact that the Imperial Parliament agreed to exclude six of the nine Ulster counties from the Free State was an acknowledgement, however reluctantly, of the right of the people of Ulster to maintain their British citizenship and membership of the Union. . . .

The modern UVF operated outside those parameters because the nature of the conflict dictated by the IRA could not be responded to effectively within the Rule of Law or within the sensitivities of civic society.

While the leaders of political and civic unionism have generally disassociated themselves from the UVF it must be said that certain of their number have made calls for the establishment of irregular loyalist militias during the past thirty years and have used the threat of a loyalist paramilitary backlash as a political bargaining chip. It should also be noted that there have been times when the wider community has supported loyalist violence. Anthony Alcock refers to a telephone poll of some 4,000 people undertaken by the Newsletter in the Spring of 1993 which showed that 42 percent declared their support for paramilitary violence, 50.2 percent answered "yes" to the question as to whether there were current circumstances in which loyalist paramilitary violence was justified, and 81 percent stated that loyalist violence was a reaction to PIRA violence and would cease if the PIRA called off its campaign. . . .

The Ulster Volunteer Force and Red Hand Commando called a ceasefire on 14th October 1994. Both organisations believed then, and continue to believe, that the cessation of armed hostilities by mainstream republicanism should be matched by a cessation of loyalist hostilities.

One of the key considerations that led the UVF/RHC leadership to endorse the 1994 cessation was a belief that the Republican Movement was questioning its continued commitment to the "armed struggle" and that a republican cessation required a measured response from loyalists. A second consideration was an acceptance by the UVF/RHC leadership that Her Majesty's Government had not entered into an agreement with the Republican Movement and/or the wider republican nationalist constituency to impose a political settlement on the people of Northern Ireland that weakened the Union or the democratic structures through which the people of Northern Ireland could determine their own political and constitutional destiny.

In the absence of republican violence the UVF/RHC leadership has seen its role as monitoring the military activity of both the Republican Movement and so-called republican dissidents. Until there is a clear and unequivocal declaration that the "war is over" the leadership of the UVF/RHC believes there is a need for it to keep a watching brief on republican activity. Both organisations will also continue to monitor the political situation to ensure that no political or constitutional settlement is imposed by either Her Majesty's Government alone, or in collaboration with the Government of the Irish Republic, that would weaken either the Union or the democratic structures through which the people of Northern Ireland can determine their own destiny.

The military structure of the Ulster Volunteer Force and Red Hand Commando will remain in place so long as a return to the "armed struggle" by mainstream republicanism, an escalation of dissident republican activity, or the threat of an imposed solution remains a possibility. . . .

Republican violence was aimed at making the continued link with the rest of the United Kingdom more oppressive for unionists than any fears they may have had about an oppressive life in a United Ireland. *What republicans regarded as the armed struggle against British imperialism, unionists regarded as a campaign of terror against them.* Even the campaign against the RUC and the British army was regarded by unionists as a campaign against them. Republicans may tell us that they merely attack a "uniform" which they regard as the symbol of British repression. Unionists look at the "uniform" and see a British citizen—one of our people—who has been tasked to protect them against republican aggression. . . .

Loyalists have never accepted the argument that the IRA campaign was a war of national liberation in which the main protagonists were the Irish people and the British State. The 1969–1974 conflict was a conflict between two peoples living side by side in Northern Ireland, not a conflict between one indigenous people and a foreign state. Loyalists regarded the republican campaign as a campaign against the unionist people and they regarded their campaign as a campaign against the nationalist people. It was a civil war, albeit an unconventional one, in which the main protagonists were the unionist and the nationalist communities, and in which the majority of casualties were civilians. . . .

If we are to avoid going back to a war in which civilians from both communities are going to be the prime sufferers we need to memorise the following words from the statement read out at the declaration of the loyalist cease-fires in October 1994:—"Let us firmly resolve to respect our differing views of freedom, culture and aspiration and never again permit our political circumstances to degenerate into bloody warfare." Until such times as the appropriate structures are put in place that allow all parties to the conflict to make the sentiments of that statement a reality, *calls for disarmament and demobilisation are unrealistic.* The process that leads to decommissioning and demobilisation must take place in tandem with the development of genuine trust and mutual respect between the several parties formerly engaged in the conflict. It is important too that this trust and respect has had time to percolate down to the ordinary members of both the nationalist and the unionist communities so as to alleviate any lingering fears and suspicions about each other's long-term intentions.

SECTION C. COMPETING CONCEPTS OF NATIONALISM: NATIONALISM AND REPUBLICANISM

10. Irish Nationalism: Excerpts from the Writings of Patrick Pearse, 1913–1916

Patrick Pearse was an educator, poet, and one of the leaders of the Irish Nationalist movement. He was also a director of the Gaelic League, which promoted the resurrection of the Irish language. Pearse founded St. Enda's College near Dublin to teach Irish traditions and culture. He commanded the Irish Republican Brotherhood and the Irish Volunteers in the Easter Rising of 1916. In these writings from 1913 to 1916 he attempted to explain the spiritual basis of Irish nationalism.

Sources: "Pádraic Pearse: Essays and Lectures," CELT: Corpus of Electronic Texts, accessed 19 February 2020, https://celt.ucc.ie/published/E900007-003, https://celt.ucc.ie/published/E900007-010, and https://celt.ucc.ie/published/E900007-012.

"The Coming Revolution" (1913)

I often said (quoting, I think, Herbert Spencer) that education should be a preparation for complete living; and I say now that our Gaelic League education ought to have been a preparation for our complete living as Irish Nationalists. In proportion as we have been faithful and diligent Gaelic Leaguers, our work as *Irish Nationalists (by which term I mean people who accept the ideal of, and work for, the realisation of an Irish Nation, by whatever means)* will be earnest and thorough, a valiant and worthy fighting, not the mere carrying out of a ritual. As to what your work as an Irish Nationalist is to be, I cannot conjecture; I know what mine is to be, and would have you know yours and buckle yourself to it. And it may be (nay, it is) that yours and mine will lead us to a common meeting place . . . ready for a greater adventure than any of us has yet had, a triumph to be endured and achieved in common. . . .

It is evident that there can be no peace between the body politic and a foreign substance that has intruded itself into its system: *between them war only until the foreign substance is expelled or assimilated.*

Whether Home Rule means a loosening or a tightening of England's grip upon Ireland remains yet to be seen. But the coming of Home Rule, if come it does, will make no material difference in the nature of the work that lies before us: it will affect only the means we are to employ, our plan of campaign. There remains, under Home Rule as in its absence, the substantial task of achieving the Irish Nation. I do not think it is going to be achieved without stress and trial, without suffering and bloodshed. . . .

A thing that stands demonstrable is that *nationhood is not achieved otherwise than in arms*: in one or two instances there may have been no actual bloodshed, but the arms were there and the ability to use them. Ireland unarmed will attain just as much freedom as it is convenient for England to give her; *Ireland armed will attain ultimately just as much freedom as she wants.* . . .

I should like to see any and every body of Irish citizens armed. We must accustom ourselves to the thought of arms, to the sight of arms, to the use of arms. We may make mistakes in the beginning and shoot the wrong people; but *bloodshed is a cleansing and a sanctifying thing*, and the nation which regards it as the final horror has lost its manhood. *There are many things more horrible than bloodshed; and slavery is one of them.*

"Ghosts" (1915)

Here be ghosts that I have raised this Christmastide, ghosts of dead men that have bequeathed a trust to us living men. . . . The ghosts of a nation sometimes ask very big things; and they must be appeased, whatever the cost. . . .

The men who have led Ireland for twenty-five years have done evil, and they are bankrupt. They are bankrupt in policy, bankrupt in credit, bankrupt now even in words. . . .

They have conceived of nationality as a material thing, whereas it is a spiritual thing. They have made the same mistake that a man would make if he were to forget that he has an immortal soul. They have not recognised in their people the image and likeness of God. Hence, the nation to them is not all holy, a thing inviolate and inviolable, a thing that a man dare not sell or dishonour on pain of eternal perdition. They have thought of nationality as a thing to be negotiated about as men negotiate a tariff or about a trade route, rather than as an immediate jewel to be preserved at all peril, a thing so sacred that it may not be brought into the market places at all or spoken of where men traffic.

He who builds on lies rears only lies. The untruth that nationality is corporeal, a thing defined by statutes and guaranteed by mutual interests, is at the base of the untruth that freedom, which is the condition of a hale nationality, is a status to be conceded rather than a glory to be achieved; and of the other untruth that it can ever be lawful in the interest of empire, in the interest of wealth, in the interest of quiet living, to forego the right to freedom. The contrary is the truth. *Freedom, being a spiritual necessity, transcends all corporeal necessities*, and when freedom is being considered interests should not be spoken of. Or, if the terms of the countinghouse be the ones that are best understood, let us put it that *it is the highest interest of a nation to be free.*

Like a divine religion, national freedom bears the marks of unity, of sanctity, of catholicity, of apostolic succession. Of unity, for it contemplates the nation as one; of sanctity, for it is holy in itself and in those who serve it; of catholicity, for it embraces all the men and women of the nation; of apostolic succession, for it, or the aspiration after it, passes down from generation to generation from the nation's fathers. A nation's fundamental idea of freedom is not affected by the accidents of time and circumstance. It does not vary with the centuries, or with the comings and goings of men or of empires. The substance of truth does not change, nor does the substance of freedom. . . .

The Irish mind is the clearest mind that has ever applied itself to the consideration of nationality and of national freedom. . . .

Irish nationality is an ancient spiritual tradition, one of the oldest and most august traditions in the world. Politically, Ireland's claim has been for freedom in order to *[experience]* the full and perpetual life of that tradition. The generations of Ireland have gone into battle for no other thing. To the Irish mind for more than a thousand years freedom has had but one definition. It has meant not a limited freedom, a freedom conditioned by the interests of another nation, a freedom compatible with the suzerain authority of a foreign parliament, but absolute freedom, the sovereign control of Irish destinies. It has not meant the freedom of a class, but the freedom of a people. *It has not meant the freedom of a geographical fragment of Ireland, but the freedom of all Ireland, of every sod of Ireland.*

And the freedom thus defined has seemed to the Irish the most desirable of all earthly things. They have valued it more than land, more than wealth, more than ease, more than empire. . . .

I make the contention that the national demand of Ireland is fixed and determined; that that demand has been made by every generation; that we of this generation receive it as a trust from our fathers; that we are bound by it; that we have not the right to alter it or to abate it by one jot or tittle; and that any undertaking made in the name of Ireland to accept in full satisfaction of Ireland's claim anything less than the generations of Ireland have stood for is null and void, binding on Ireland neither by the law of God nor by the law of nations.

"The Spiritual Nation" (1916)

I believe *that there is really a spiritual tradition which is the soul of Ireland*, the thing which makes Ireland a living nation, and that there is such a spiritual tradition corresponding to every true nationality. . . .

Davis [Thomas] was the first of modern Irishmen to make explicit the truth that a nationality is a spirituality . . . that Ireland must be herself, not merely a free self-governing state, but authentically the Irish nation, bearing all the majestic marks of her nationhood. *That the nation may live, the Irish Life, both the inner life and the outer life, must be conserved. Hence the language, which is the main repository of the Irish life, the folklore, the literature, the music, the art, the social customs, must be preserved.* Davis fully realized with the Gaelic poets, that a nationality connotes a civilization and that a civilization is a body of traditions. . . .

Ireland is one. Tone had insisted upon the political unity of Ireland. Davis thought of Ireland as a spiritual unity. He recognized that the thing which makes her one is her history, that all her men and women are heirs of a common past, a past full of spiritual, emotional, and intellectual experiences, which knits them together indissolubly. The nation is thus not a mere agglomeration of individuals, but a living, organic thing, with a body and a soul; twofold in nature, like man, yet one.

11. The Easter Rising Proclamation, 1916

The Easter Proclamation was written by James Connolly, Patrick Pearse, and the other members of the "Provisional Government of Ireland" and was read out by Pearse on the steps of the General Post Office in Dublin as part of the Easter Rising. It proclaimed Ireland's independence from England and is seen by Nationalists as the origin of the Irish Republic.

Source: "Politics," CAIN, accessed 1 July 2019, https://cain.ulster.ac.uk/issues/politics/docs/pir24416.

POBLACHT NA H EIREANN.
THE PROVISIONAL GOVERNMENT OF THE IRISH REPUBLIC TO THE PEOPLE OF IRELAND.

IRISHMEN AND IRISHWOMEN: In the name of God and of the dead generations from which she receives her old tradition of nationhood, Ireland, through us, summons her children to her flag and strikes for her freedom.

Having organised and trained her manhood through her secret revolutionary organisation, the Irish Republican Brotherhood, and through her open military organisations, the Irish Volunteers and the Irish Citizen Army, having patiently perfected her discipline, having resolutely waited for the right moment to reveal itself, she now seizes that moment, and supported by her exiled children in America and by gallant allies in Europe, but relying in the first on her own strength, she strikes in full confidence of victory.

We declare the right of the people of Ireland to the ownership of Ireland and to the unfettered control of Irish destinies, to be sovereign and indefeasible. The long usurpation of that right by a foreign people and government has not extinguished the right, nor can it ever be extinguished except by the destruction of the Irish people. *In every generation the Irish people have asserted their right to national freedom and sovereignty*; six times during the past three hundred years they have asserted it in arms. Standing on that fundamental right and again asserting it in arms in the face of the world, *we hereby proclaim the Irish Republic as a Sovereign Independent State*, and we pledge our lives and the lives of our comrades in arms to the cause of its freedom, of its welfare, and of its exaltation among the nations.

The Irish Republic is entitled to, and hereby claims, the allegiance of every Irishman and Irishwoman. The Republic guarantees religious and civil liberty, equal rights and equal opportunities to all its citizens, and declares its resolve to pursue the happiness and prosperity of the whole nation and of all its parts, cherishing all of the children of the nation equally, and oblivious of the differences carefully fostered by an alien Government, which have divided a minority from the majority in the past.

Until our arms have brought the opportune moment for the establishment of a permanent National Government, representative of the whole people of Ireland and elected by the suffrages of all her men and women, the Provisional Government, hereby constituted, will administer the civil and military affairs of the Republic in trust for the people.

We place the cause of the Irish Republic under the protection of the Most High God, Whose blessing we invoke upon our arms, and we pray that no one who serves that cause will dishonour it by cowardice, inhumanity, or rapine. In this supreme hour the Irish nation must, by its valour and discipline, and by the readiness of its children to sacrifice themselves for the common good, prove itself worthy of the august destiny to which it is called.

Signed on behalf of the Provisional Government,
THOMAS J. CLARKE
SEAN MAC DIARMADA
P. H. PEARSE
JAMES CONNOLLY
THOMAS MACDONAGH
EAMONN CEANNT
JOSEPH PLUNKETT

12. Excerpt from the Constitution of Ireland, Adopted 1937

This constitution, written by the Irish taoiseach, Eamon de Valera, and his party, Fianna Fáil, was written and passed by a popular referendum in order to clearly establish a separate Irish identity and remove Ireland further from the constitution of the Irish Free State, which they saw as being imposed by Britain in 1922. Unionists in Northern Ireland were particularly concerned about the constitution's claim to the whole island of Ireland.

Source: "Constitution of Ireland," Wikisource, accessed 1 July 2019, https://en.wikisource.org/wiki/Constitution_of_Ireland_(original_text)

PREAMBLE

In the Name of the Most Holy Trinity, from Whom is all authority and to Whom, as our final end, all actions both of men and States must be referred,

We, the people of Éire,

Humbly acknowledging all our obligations to our Divine Lord, Jesus Christ, Who sustained our fathers through centuries of trial,

Gratefully remembering their heroic and unremitting struggle to regain the rightful independence of our Nation,

And seeking to promote the common good, with due observance of Prudence, Justice and Charity, so that the dignity and freedom of the individual may be assured, true social order attained, the unity of our country restored, and concord established with other nations,

Do hereby adopt, enact, and give to ourselves this Constitution.

THE NATION
ARTICLE 1

The Irish nation hereby affirms its inalienable, indefeasible, and sovereign right to choose its own form of Government, to determine its relations with other nations, and to develop its life, political, economic and cultural, in accordance with its own genius and traditions.

ARTICLE 2

The national territory consists of the whole island of Ireland, its islands and the territorial seas.

ARTICLE 3

Pending the re-integration of the national territory, and without prejudice to the right of the Parliament and Government established by this Constitution to exercise jurisdiction over the whole of that territory, the laws enacted by that Parliament shall have the like area and extent of application as the laws of Saorstát Éireann and the like extra-territorial effect.

THE STATE
ARTICLE 4

The name of the State is Éire, or, in the English language, Ireland.

ARTICLE 5

Ireland is a sovereign, independent, democratic state.

ARTICLE 44 1.2

The State recognizes the special position of the Holy Catholic Apostolic and Roman Church as the guardian of the Faith professed by the great majority of the citizens.

ARTICLE 44 2.1
Freedom of conscience and the free profession of and practice of religion are, subject to public order and morality, guaranteed for every citizen.

13. Eamon de Valera's Vision of the Irish Republic, 1943

Excerpt from a radio address by the Irish taoiseach (one of the IRA commanders in 1916), Eamon de Valera, "On Language and the Irish Nation," 17 May 1943.

Source: Maurice Moynihan, ed., *Speeches and Statements by Eamon de Valera, 1917-1973* (Dublin: Gill and Macmillan, 1980), 466.

The ideal Ireland that we would have, the Ireland that we dreamed of, would be the home of a people who valued material wealth only as a basis for right living, of a people who, satisfied with frugal comfort, devoted their leisure to the things of the spirit—a land whose countryside would be bright with cosy homesteads, whose fields and villages would be joyous with the sounds of industry, with the romping of sturdy children, the contest of athletic youths and the laughter of happy maidens, whose firesides would be forums for the wisdom of serene old age. The home, in short, of a people living the life that God desires that men should live. With the tidings that make such an Ireland possible, St. Patrick came to our ancestors fifteen hundred years ago promising happiness here no less than happiness hereafter. It was the pursuit of such an Ireland that later made our country worthy to be called the island of saints and scholars. It was the idea of such an Ireland—happy, vigorous, spiritual—that fired the imagination of our poets; that made successive generations of patriotic men give their lives to win religious and political liberty; and that will urge men in our own and future generations to die, if need be, so that these liberties may be preserved. One hundred years ago, the Young Irelanders, by holding up the vision of such an Ireland before the people, inspired and moved them spiritually as our people had hardly been moved since the Golden Age of Irish civilisation. Fifty years later, the founders of the Gaelic League similarly inspired and moved the people of their day. So, later, did the leaders of the Irish Volunteers. We of this time, if we have the will and active enthusiasm, have the opportunity to inspire and move our generation in like manner. We can do so by keeping this thought of a noble future for our country constantly before our eyes, ever seeking in action to bring that future into being, and ever remembering that it is for our nation as a whole that future must be sought.

14. Excerpt from *Northern Ireland: The Plain Truth*, 2nd ed., 1969

This pamphlet was issued on 15 June 1969 by the Campaign for Social Justice in Northern Ireland, one of the groups leading the civil rights campaign.

Source: "Civil Rights Campaign," CAIN, accessed 19 July 2019, https://cain.ulster.ac.uk/events/crights/pdfs/truth.pdf.

Since 1920, when Ireland was divided, the Republic of Ireland has been a separate independent state, while Northern Ireland has remained an integral part of the United Kingdom. It is now loosely termed "Ulster" although there were nine counties in old-time Ulster, three of which are now in the Republic of Ireland. The British Parliament in London first legalised this arrangement by the Government of Ireland Act, 1920 (H. M. Stationery Office, London). London has since ruled Northern Ireland through its subordinate Parliament at Stormont, Belfast.

Both London and Stormont have always been at pains to present the province as a happy, contented place, *whereas in fact it contains a minority which has always been very hard pressed, and indeed denied rights which most of the free world has come to accept as a matter of course.*

The outside world was largely unaware of what was going on in Ulster mainly because the British press had always been discouraged from printing stories about it. Some years ago when a British television group had a series of documentaries suppressed, the leader of the reporting team, Alan Whicker, declared "No country deserves the Government you have here. This is the only place in the world where you can't report honestly without silly people kicking up about what is only the truth."

Since the 5th October, 1968, when a peaceful Civil Rights march was broken up by the police, the world has been looking at Northern Ireland on television, and reading about her in the press, first with incredulity, and then shock.

Civil Rights activities have been opposed by various groups of militant Protestants. These people already have their civil rights, and do not wish to share them with others. They have caused the recent unrest by opposing democratic demands for change. This opposition has been effected mainly by violent counter-demonstrations, and by arbitrary police bans on Civil Rights marches in certain places, e.g., in the city of Londonderry.

This booklet attempts to explain the situation in Northern Ireland, and to detail the discriminatory injustices from which the minority has been suffering there for almost fifty years.

There are roughly one and a half million people living in Northern Ireland, of whom two thirds are Protestant, and who generally support the Unionist Government. The remaining one third are Roman Catholics, who generally support a variety of opposition parties.

Out of a total of 52, the Unionists hold 39 seats in the Stormont Parliament. They are closely linked with the Conservative (Tory) party in Britain. The Unionist Party is a sectarian one. Down the years it has discouraged Catholics from joining and at present only a dozen or so belong to it. It is dominated by the Orange Order, a secret society having many points of similarity with the Dutch Reformed Church in South Africa. Virtually all of the Government, including the present Prime Minister, Major Chichester-Clark as well as most Unionist parliamentarians, are members of the Orange Order. Six Nationalists, four Labour and three Independent members make up the Parliamentary opposition.

Northern Ireland also sends twelve M.P.'s to the London Parliament (Westminster). For many years they were all Unionists, boosting Conservative voting strength there. This is a main reason why the British Conservatives, who were in power most of the time, did not insist that the Stormont Government should modify their repressive and discriminatory policies towards the political minority. One of these London seats was taken from the Unionists in 1964, and is now held by the redoubtable Gerry Fitt. In April 1969, a twenty-one year old Civil Rights leader, Bernadette Devlin, took another seat from the Unionists to become the youngest M.P. in the London Parliament.

15. The IRA Green Book: Guerrilla Strategy, 1977

The IRA Green Book was a training and induction manual issued to all new recruits. It explained the IRA's purpose, mission and methods, stressing the need for secrecy and commitment. This extract from the 1977 edition explains the IRA's strategy of guerrilla warfare.

Source: "The IRA Green Book," Alpha History, accessed 1 July 2019, https://alphahistory.com/northernireland/ira-green-book-guerrilla-1977.

Many figures of speech have been used to describe guerrilla warfare, one of the most apt being "The War of the Flea," which conjures up the image of a flea harrying a creature of elephantine size into fleeing (forgive the pun). *Thus it is with a guerrilla army such as the IRA, which employs hit and run tactics against the Brits, while at the same time striking at the soft economic underbelly of the enemy—not with the hope of physically driving them into the sea but nevertheless expecting to effect their withdrawal by an effective campaign of continuing harassment,* contained in a fivefold guerrilla strategy:

1. A War of attrition against enemy personnel which is aimed at causing as many casualties and deaths as possible, so as to create a demand from their people at home for their withdrawal.
2. A bombing campaign aimed at making the enemy's financial interest in our country unprofitable, while at the same time curbing long term financial investment in our country.
3. To make the Six Counties . . . ungovernable except by colonial military rule.
4. To sustain the war and gain support for its end using national and international propaganda and publicity campaigns.
5. By defending the war of liberation by punishing criminals, collaborators and informers.

While one of OUR chief considerations in deciding tactics is the concern for our friends, relatives, neighbours, our people in the midst of whom we operate, the enemy is simply dealing with an impersonal, inferior foreigner—a "Paddy," "Musck-Savage" or "Bog-Wog"— and with the great added advantage of all the resources and back up of a conventional army [and] paramilitary police. . . .

At this juncture the most obvious differences between the [British soldier] and the IRA volunteer, apart from the fact that *the Brit is an uninvited armed foreigner who has no moral or historical justification for being here in the first place*, are those of support, motivation and freedom of personal initiative. . . .

His billets, dumps, weapons, wages, etc., are all as stated earlier provided for by involuntary taxation. His people who pay the taxes have never indicated, nor indeed have they been asked to indicate by any democratic means, their assent to his being here at their expense. The IRA volunteer receives all his support voluntarily from his people.

A member of the IRA is such by his own choice, his convictions being the only factor which compels him to volunteer, his objectives [are] political freedom and social and economic justice for his people. Apart from the few minutes in the career of the average Brit that he comes under attack, the Brit has no freedom or personal initiative. He is told when to sleep, where to sleep, when to get up, where to spend his free time. The IRA volunteer, except when carrying out a specific army task, acts most of the time on his own initiative and must therefore shoulder that responsibility. . . .

By now it is clear that our task is not only to kill as many enemy personnel as possible but, of equal importance, to create support which will carry us though not just a war of liberation [but] past the "Brits Out" stage to the ultimate aim of a democratic-socialist republic.

SECTION D. DOCUMENTS ON THE MULTIPARTY TALKS

16. Joint Declaration on Peace: The Downing Street Declaration, 1993

The Downing Street Declaration, excerpted here, was issued on Wednesday, 15 December 1993, by the British prime minister, John Major, and the Irish taoiseach, Albert Reynolds, after years of secret negotiations in which John Hume and Gerry Adams were consulting with the Dublin government. It laid the groundwork for the peace negotiations by finding a way to encapsulate both the concepts of self-determination for the people of Ireland and the principle of consent for the citizens of Northern Ireland.

Source: "Irish Peace Process: List of Source Documents," CAIN, accessed 23 April 2019, https://cain.ulster.ac.uk/events/peace/docs/dsd151293.

1. The Taoiseach, Mr. Albert Reynolds, TD and the Prime Minister, the Rt. Hon. John Major MP, acknowledge that the most urgent and important issue facing the people of Ireland, North and South, and the British and Irish Governments together, is to remove the conflict, to overcome the legacy of history and to heal the divisions which have resulted, recognising the absence of a lasting and satisfactory settlement of relationships between the peoples of both islands has contributed to continuing tragedy and suffering. They believe that the development of an agreed framework for peace, which has been discussed between them since early last year, and which is based on a number of key principles articulated by the two Governments over the past 20 years, together with adaptation of other widely accepted principles, provides the starting point of a peace process designed to culminate in a political settlement.

2. The Taoiseach and the Prime Minister are convinced of the inestimable value to both their peoples, and particularly for the next generation, of healing divisions in Ireland and of ending a conflict which has been so manifestly to the detriment of all. Both recognise that the ending of divisions can come about only through the agreement and co-operation of the people, North and South, representing both traditions in Ireland. They therefore make a solemn commitment to promote co-operation at all levels on the basis of the fundamental principles, undertakings, obligations under international agreements, to which they have jointly committed themselves, and the guarantees which each Government has given and now reaffirms, including Northern Ireland's statutory constitutional guarantee. It is their aim to foster agreement and reconciliation, leading to a new political framework founded on consent and encompassing arrangements within Northern Ireland, for the whole island, and between these islands.

3. They also consider that the development of Europe will, of itself, require new approaches to serve interests common to both parts of the island of Ireland, and to Ireland and the United Kingdom as partners in the European Union.

4. The Prime Minister, on behalf of the British Government, reaffirms that they will uphold the democratic wish of the greater number of the people of Northern Ireland on the issue of whether they prefer to support the Union or a sovereign united Ireland. On this basis, he reiterates, on the behalf of the British Government, that they have no selfish strategic or economic interest in Northern Ireland. Their primary interest is to see peace, stability and reconciliation established by agreement among all the people inhabit the island, and they will work together with the Irish Government to achieve such an agreement, which will embrace the totality of relationships. The role of the British Government will be to encourage, facilitate and enable the achievement of such agreement over a period through a process of dialogue and co-operation based on full respect for the rights and identities of both traditions in Ireland. They accept that such agreement may, as of right, take the form of agreed structures for the island as a whole, including a united Ireland achieved by peaceful means on the following basis. The British Government agree that it is for the people of the island of Ireland alone, by agreement between the two parts respectively, to exercise their right of self-determination on the basis of consent, freely and concurrently given, North and South, to bring about a united Ireland, if that is their wish. . . .

5. The Taoiseach, on behalf of the Irish Government, considers that the lessons of Irish history, and especially of Northern Ireland, show that stability and well-being will not be found under any political system which is refused allegiance or rejected on grounds of identity by a significant minority of those governed by it. For this reason, it would be wrong to attempt to impose a united Ireland, in the absence of the freely given consent of the majority of the people of Northern Ireland. He accepts, on behalf of the Irish Government, that the democratic right of self-determination by the people of Ireland as a whole must be achieved and exercised with and subject to the agreement and consent of a majority of the people of Northern Ireland and must, consistent with justice and equity, respect the democratic dignity and the civil rights and religious liberties of both communities, including:

- the right of free political thought;
- the right of freedom and expression of religion;
- the right to pursue democratically national and political aspirations;
- the right to seek constitutional change by peaceful and legitimate means;
- the right to live wherever one chooses without hindrance;
- the right to equal opportunity in all social and economic activity, regardless of class, creed, sex or colour.

These would be reflected in any future political and constitutional arrangements emerging from a new and more broadly based agreement.

6. The Taoiseach however recognises the genuine difficulties and barriers to building relationships of trust either within or beyond Northern Ireland, from which both traditions suffer. He will work to create a new era of trust, in which suspicion of the motives and actions of others is removed on the part of either community. He considers that the future of the island depends on the nature of the relationship between the two main traditions that inhabit it. Every effort must be made to build a new series of trust between those communities. . . . The Taoiseach hopes that over time a meeting of hearts and minds will develop, which will bring all the people of Ireland together, and will work towards that objective, but he pledges in the meantime that as a result of the efforts that will be made to build mutual confidence no Northern Unionist should ever have a fear in future that this ideal will be pursued either by threat or coercion.

7. Both Governments accept that Irish unity would be achieved only by those who favour this outcome persuading those who do not, peacefully and without coercion or violence, and that, if in the future a majority of the people of Northern Ireland are so persuaded, both Governments will support and give legislative effect to their wish. But, notwithstanding the solemn affirmation by both Governments in the Anglo-Irish Agreement that any change in the status of Northern Ireland, would only come about with a consent of the majority of the people of Northern Ireland, the Taoiseach also recognises the continuing uncertainties and misgivings which dominate so much of Northern Unionist attitudes towards the rest of Ireland. He believes that we stand at a stage of our history when the genuine feelings of all traditions in the North must be recognised and acknowledged. He appeals to both traditions at this time to grasp the opportunity for a fresh start and a new beginning, which could hold such promise for all our lives and the generations to come. He asks the people of Northern Ireland to look on the people of the Republic as friends, who share their grief and shame over all the suffering of the last quarter of a century, and who wants to develop the best possible relationship with them, a relationship in which trust and new understanding can flourish and grow. The Taoiseach also acknowledges the presence in the Constitution of the Republic of elements which are deeply resented by Northern Unionists, but which at the same time reflect hopes and ideals which lie deep in the hearts of many Irish men and women North and South. But as we move towards a new era of understanding in new relationships of trust may grow and bring peace to the island of Ireland, the Taoiseach believes that the time has come to consider together how best the hopes and identities of all can be expressed in more balanced ways, which no longer engender division and the lack of trust to which he has referred. He confirms that, in the event of an overall settlement, the Irish Government will, as part of a balanced constitutional accommodation, put forward and support proposals for change in the Irish Constitution which would fully reflect the principle of consent in Northern Ireland. . . .

10. The British and Irish Governments reiterate that the achievement of peace must involve a permanent end to the use of, or support for, paramilitary violence. They confirm that, in these circumstances, democratically mandated parties which establish a commitment to exclusively peaceful methods and which have shown that they abide by the democratic process, are free to participate fully in democratic politics and to join in dialogue in due course between the Governments and the political parties on the way ahead.

17. The Paramilitary Ceasefire Announcements, 1994

The IRA Declares a Ceasefire (August 1994)

Source: "The 1994 Ceasefire," Alpha History, accessed 1 July 2019, https://alphahistory.com/northernireland/ira-declares-ceasefire-1994.

On August 31st 1994 the Provisional IRA released the following statement, declaring an indefinite ceasefire pending further peace negotiations. The ceasefire would be broken the following year with the detonation of a massive truck bomb in London:

> Recognizing the potential of the current situation and in order to enhance the democratic process and underlying our definitive commitment to its success, the leadership of the IRA have decided that as of midnight there will be a complete cessation of military operations. All our units have been instructed accordingly.
>
> At this crossroads the leadership of the IRA salutes and commends our volunteers, other activists, our supporters and the political prisoners who have sustained the struggle against all odds for the past 25 years. Your courage, determination and sacrifice have demonstrated that the freedom and the desire for peace based on a just and lasting settlement cannot be crushed. We remember all those who have died for Irish freedom and we reiterate our commitment to our republican objectives. Our struggle has seen many gains and advances made by nationalists and for the democratic position.
>
> We believe that an opportunity to secure a just and lasting settlement has been created. We are therefore entering into a new situation in a spirit of determination and confidence, determined that the injustices which created this conflict will be removed and confident in the strength and justice of our struggle to achieve this.

We note that the Downing Street Declaration is not a solution, nor was it presented as such by its authors. A solution will only be found as a result of inclusive negotiations. Others, not the least the British government have a duty to face up to their responsibilities. It is our desire to significantly contribute to the creation of a climate which will encourage this. We urge everyone to approach this new situation with energy, determination and patience."

Loyalist Paramilitary Groups Declare a Ceasefire (October 1994)

Source: "1994 Ceasefire," Alpha History, accessed 1 July 2019, https://alphahistory.com/northernireland/loyalist-paramilitary-groups-ceasefire-1994.

In October 1994 the Combined Loyalist Military Command [CLMC], an umbrella group representing several Loyalist paramilitary groups, issued the following ceasefire statement:

After a widespread consultative process initiated by representations from the Ulster Democratic and Progressive Unionist Parties, and after having received confirmation and guarantees in relation to Northern Ireland's constitutional position within the United Kingdom, as well as other assurances, and, in the belief that the democratically expressed wishes of the greater number of people in Northern Ireland will be respected and upheld, the CLMC will universally cease all operational hostilities as from midnight on Thursday October 13th 1994.

The permanence of our ceasefire will be completely dependant [*sic*] upon the continued cessation of all nationalist-republican violence, the sole responsibility for a return to war lies with them.

In the genuine hope that this peace will be permanent, we take the opportunity to pay homage to all our fighters, commandos and volunteers who paid the supreme sacrifice. They did not die in vain. The Union is safe.

To our physically and mentally wounded who have served Ulster so unselfishly, we wish a speedy recovery, and to the relatives of these men and women, we pledge our continued moral and practical support.

To our prisoners who have undergone so much deprivation and degradation with great courage and forbearance, we solemnly promise to leave no stone unturned to secure their freedom . . .

In all sincerity, we offer to the loved ones of all innocent victims over the past twenty years, abject and true remorse. No words of ours will compensate for the intolerable suffering they have undergone during the conflict.

Let us firmly resolve to respect our differing views of freedom, culture and aspiration and never again permit our political circumstances to degenerate into bloody warfare. We are on the threshold of a new and exciting beginning, with our battles in future being political battles, fought on the side of honesty, decency and democracy against the negativity of mistrust, misunderstanding and malevolence, so that together we can bring forth a wholesome society in which our children, and their children, will know the meaning of true peace.

18. Consultation Paper: Ground Rules for Substantive All-Party Negotiations Issued by the British Government, 15 March 1996

Source: "Irish Peace Process: List of Source Documents," CAIN, accessed 4 May 2019, https://cain.ulster.ac.uk/events/peace/docs/cp15396.htm.

The Basis, Participation, Structure, Format and Agenda of All-Party Negotiations

Basis

1. The purpose of the negotiations will be to achieve a new beginning for relationships within Northern Ireland, among the people of the island of Ireland and between the peoples of these islands, and to agree new institutions and structures to take account of the totality of relationships.

Agenda

2. The negotiations will, therefore, in a full and comprehensive fashion, address and seek to reach agreement on relationships and arrangements within Northern Ireland, including the relationship between any new institutions there and the Westminster Parliament; within the whole island of Ireland; and between the two Governments, including their relationship with any new institutions in Northern Ireland.

3. Any participant will be free to raise any aspect of the three relationships, including constitutional issues and any other matter which it considers relevant. While no outcome is either predetermined or excluded in advance, and while participation in negotiations is without prejudice to any participant's commitment to the achievement by exclusively peaceful and democratic means of its own preferred options, it is common ground that any agreement, if it is to command widespread support, will need to give adequate expression to the totality of all three relationships.

Structure

5. Negotiations will be structured through a coordinated and interlocking three-stranded format. Strand One will cover relationships within Northern Ireland; Strand Two will cover relationships within the island of Ireland and Strand Three will cover relationships between the British and Irish Governments.

Participation

7. In the communique of 28 February, both Governments expressed the hope that all parties with an electoral mandate will be able to participate in all-party negotiations. However, both Governments are also agreed that the resumption of Ministerial dialogue with Sinn Féin, and their participation in negotiations, requires the unequivocal restoration of the ceasefire of August 1994.

Opening of Negotiations

10. In their Communique of 28 February, the Taoiseach and the Prime Minister said that "they recognise that confidence building measures will be necessary. As one such measure, all participants would need to make clear at the beginning of the discussions their total and absolute commitment to the principles of democracy and non-violence set out in the report of the International Body. They would also need to address, at that stage, its proposals on decommissioning. Confidence building would also require that the parties have reassurance that a meaningful and inclusive process of negotiations is genuinely being offered to address the legitimate concerns of their traditions and the need for new political arrangements with which all can identify."

12. Both Governments are determined that the structure and process of the negotiations will be used in the most constructive possible manner in the search for agreement. They will use their influence in the appropriate strands to ensure that all items on the comprehensive agenda are fully addressed in the negotiating process and commit themselves, for their part, to doing so with a view to overcoming any obstacles which may arise. All participants in the negotiations will take part in good faith, seriously address all aspects of the agreed agenda, and make every effort to reach agreement. They will maintain confidentiality on all aspects of the negotiations except where they may from time to time agree to publicity.

13. If, during the negotiations, any party demonstrably dishonoured its commitment to the principles of democracy and non-violence by, for example, resorting to force or threatening the use of force to influence the course or the outcome of the negotiations, or failing to oppose the efforts of others to do so, it would no longer be entitled to participate in the negotiations.

Format

19. The negotiations will proceed on the shared understanding that nothing will be finally agreed in any strand until everything is agreed in the negotiations as a whole. It would nevertheless be possible solely on the basis of consensus among the participants to reach contingent agreement on individual aspects.20. The negotiations will operate on the basis of consensus. However, if in Strand One or Two it

should prove impossible after determined efforts to achieve unanimity, the Chairperson may, without prejudice to the provisions of the previous paragraph, operate on the basis of sufficient consensus among the political parties to allow negotiations to proceed. . . .

The overall outcome across all three strands would also need to attract a sufficient consensus from the participants.

Validation 22
Both Governments reaffirm their intention that the outcome of negotiations will be submitted for public approval by referendums in Ireland—North and South—before being submitted to their respective Parliaments for ratification and the earliest possible implementation.

19. The "Mitchell Principles," or "Principles of Democracy and Non-violence," 1996

These principles were recommended in the Report of the International Body on Arms Decommissioning, 22 January 1996, a body chaired by Senator George Mitchell. Participants in the multiparty talks had to agree to the principles before taking part in the talks.

Source: "Irish Peace Process: List of Source Documents," CAIN, accessed 1 July 2019, https://cain.ulster.ac.uk/events/peace/docs/gm24196.htm.

III. RECOMMENDATIONS: PRINCIPLES OF DEMOCRACY AND NON-VIOLENCE

[1]. To reach an agreed political settlement and to take the gun out of Irish politics, there must be commitment and adherence to fundamental principles of democracy and non-violence. Participants in all-party negotiations should affirm their commitment to such principles.

[2]. Accordingly, we recommend that the parties to such negotiations affirm their total and absolute commitment:

a. To democratic and exclusively peaceful means of resolving political issues;
b. To the total disarmament of all paramilitary organisations;
c. To agree that such disarmament must be verifiable to the satisfaction of an independent commission;
d. To renounce for themselves, and to oppose any effort by others, to use force, or threaten to use force, to influence the course or the outcome of all-party negotiations;
e. To agree to abide by the terms of any agreement reached in all-party negotiations and to resort to democratic and exclusively peaceful methods in trying to alter any aspect of that outcome with which they may disagree; and,
f. To urge that "punishment" killings and beatings stop and to take effective steps to prevent such actions.

[3]. We join the Governments, religious leaders and many others in condemning "punishment" killings and beatings. They contribute to the fear that those who have used violence to pursue political objectives in the past will do so again in the future. Such actions have no place in a lawful society.

[4]. Those who demand decommissioning prior to all-party negotiations do so out of concern that the paramilitaries will use force, threaten to use force, to influence the negotiations, or to change any aspect of the outcome of negotiations with which they disagree.

Given the history of Northern Ireland, this is not an unreasonable concern. The principles we recommend address those concerns directly.

[5]. These commitments, when made and honoured, would remove the threat of force before, during and after all-party negotiations. They would focus all concerned on what is ultimately essential if the gun is to be taken out of Irish politics: an agreed political settlement and the total and verifiable disarmament of all paramilitary organisations. That should encourage the belief that the peace process will truly be an exercise in democracy, not one influenced by the threat of violence.

20. Excerpts from the Charter of Fundamental Rights of the European Union, 2000

The cross-community Alliance Party and the Northern Ireland Women's Coalition as well as John Hume and the Social Democratic and Labour Party saw the possibility of easing relations between Ireland and Great Britain, as well as the competing communities in Northern Ireland, by applying the principles of the European Union to which both countries belonged.

Source: "Charter of Fundamental Rights of the European Union," EUR-LEX, assessed 1 May 2019, https://eur-lex.europa.eu/legal-content/EN/TXT/PDF/?uri=CELEX:12012P/TXT.

CHARTER OF FUNDAMENTAL RIGHTS OF THE EUROPEAN UNION

The peoples of Europe, in creating an ever closer union among them, are resolved to share a peaceful future based on common values.

Conscious of its spiritual and moral heritage, the Union is founded on the indivisible, universal values of human dignity, freedom, equality and solidarity; it is based on the principles of democracy and the rule of law. It places the individual at the heart of its activities, by establishing the citizenship of the Union and by creating an area of freedom, security and justice.

The Union contributes to the preservation and to the development of these common values while respecting the diversity of the cultures and traditions of the peoples of Europe as well as the national identities of the Member States and the organisation of their public authorities at national, regional and local levels; it seeks to promote balanced and sustainable development and ensures free movement of persons, services, goods and capital, and the freedom of establishment. . . .

The Union therefore recognises the rights, freedoms and principles set out hereafter.

Article 1: Human dignity

Human dignity is inviolable. It must be respected and protected.

Article 6: Right to liberty and security

Everyone has the right to liberty and security of person.

Article 10: Freedom of thought, conscience and religion

1. Everyone has the right to freedom of thought, conscience and religion. This right includes freedom to change religion or belief and freedom, either alone or in community with others and in public or in private, to manifest religion or belief, in worship, teaching, practice and observance.

Article 11: Freedom of expression and information

1. Everyone has the right to freedom of expression. This right shall include freedom to hold opinions and to receive and impart information and ideas without interference by public authority and regardless of frontiers.

2. The freedom and pluralism of the media shall be respected.

Article 12: Freedom of assembly and of association

1. Everyone has the right to freedom of peaceful assembly and to freedom of association at all levels, in particular in political, trade union and civic matters, which implies the right of everyone to form and to join trade unions for the protection of his or her interests.

Article 20: Equality before the law

Everyone is equal before the law.

Article 21: Non-discrimination

1. Any discrimination based on any ground such as sex, race, colour, ethnic or social origin, genetic features, language, religion or belief, political or any other opinion, membership of a national minority, property, birth, disability, age or sexual orientation shall be prohibited.

SECTION E. UNIONIST POLITICAL DOCUMENTS OF THE 1990S

21. Ian Paisley Speech to the Democratic Unionist Party's Annual Conference, 1994

The Reverend Ian Paisley was one of the founders of the Free Presbyterian Church in the 1950s and known for his condemnation of Catholicism, the civil rights movement, and Republicanism. At the time of the talks he had been the leader of the Democratic Unionist Party since he helped found it in 1971.

Source: "Irish Peace Process: List of Source Documents," CAIN, accessed 23 April 2019, https://cain.ulster.ac.uk/events/peace/soc.htm#1994.

The State of the Union

. . . I care not for the siren voices of those who will raise them against me. I care not for the strength of the opposition I only care that the blood of the people I represent will not be upon my garments in the day of final judgment before my God.

This speech could well be called the "state of the Union," that is the state, of the Union between this part of the United Kingdom Northern Ireland and the rest of the United Kingdom Great Britain.

Let us first put the birth of the Union in historical perspective. During the terrible massacre of 1641, Phelim O'Neill poured out a fiendish cruelty and torture on our Protestant forefathers for no other crime than that they were Protestants and would not bow the knee to the Papal Antichrist at the Vatican. This extermination of Protestants became from that time a contagious disease in Ireland but was cured for a time by the Williamite Revolution Settlement. The enemy's claws were cut, but they continued to grow again. The end of the 18th century witnessed another terrible tragedy: the Rebellion of 1798. In the County of Wexford, especially, the maws of Rome protruded once again from the glove of velvet, and the massacre was repeated. The horrors of Wexford Bridge and its aftermath were a second historical reminder of what would befall us if Popery were once again to gain the ascendancy in this land. *The Act of Union of 1800 was thus conceived in the spirit of defending religious liberties and civil rights.* It took effect on 1st January, 1801. It abolished the Irish Parliament and provided that Ireland was to be represented by 100 members in the British House of Commons, 28 Irish peers in the House of Lords, and 4 bishops of the established church.

The first Article of the Act of Union unites Great Britain and Ireland (now Northern Ireland) into one kingdom "for ever." This Article has as great a force as any other statutory provision, and it is by the Act of Union that Northern Ireland forms part of the United Kingdom. It is the basis of the Parliamentary sovereignty exercised by Westminster over all parts of the United Kingdom.

The Act of Union thus legally created the United Kingdom "for ever," made the provision that *its sovereignty resided solely and exclusively in Westminster, and guaranteed the ascendancy of Protestantism, the defence of the Faith.*

The famous Section 75 of the Government of Ireland Act of 1920 secured the establishment of the Parliaments of Southern and Northern Ireland but in no way impinged on the supreme authority of the United Kingdom over all persons, matters, and things in Ireland and every part thereof.

The 1921 Treaty, however, superseded the 1920 Act, providing the 26 Counties as a self-governing Dominion on which the Parliament of the United Kingdom had no claim. All references in the 1920 Act which included "all Ireland" now were defined as "Northern Ireland," thus establishing in law the unity of Northern Ireland as part of the United Kingdom. This was confirmed in the 1922 Consequential Provisions Act, which contains a modification of the 1920 Act in the following words: "the Government of Ireland Act 1920 shall cease to apply to any other part of Ireland other than Northern Ireland."

We then come to the Boundary Commission of 1925, whose forecast, which was leaked, so alarmed the Free State Government that they immediately entered into negotiations for an agreement, which was signed on 3rd December, 1925 by representatives of Great Britain, Northern Ireland, and the Irish Free State. Under Article 1 the extent of Northern Ireland, as defined by the Act of 1920, was confirmed, and consequentially the whole of the six counties (Armagh, Antrim, Down, Fermanagh, Londonderry and Tyrone) were definitely secured to Northern Ireland. This agreement was ratified by an Act of the Imperial Parliament, and also by an Act of the Irish Free State, which was number 40 in their Statute Book of the year 1925. In fact, it was accepted by overwhelming majorities of both Houses of Parliament sitting in Dublin. . . .

On 11th May, 1949, the Prime Minister Clement Atlee made a move to establish that *no change in the Constitution of Northern Ireland be made without the consent of Northern Ireland*, and that guarantee was part of the Ireland Act 1949:

> "It is hereby declared that Northern Ireland remains part of His Majesty's dominions and of the United Kingdom and it is hereby affirmed that in no event will Northern Ireland or any part thereof cease to be part of His Majesty's dominions and of the United Kingdom without the consent of the Parliament of Northern Ireland."

When the Parliament of Northern Ireland was suspended by the Heath Government, I moved in the House of Commons that Northern Ireland remains part of Her Majesty's Dominions and of the United Kingdom, and this is incorporated in the Northern Ireland Constitution Act of 1973:

> "It is hereby declared that Northern Ireland remains part of Her Majesty's dominions and of the United Kingdom, and it is hereby affirmed that in no event will Northern Ireland or any part of it cease to be part of Her Majesty's dominions and of the United Kingdom without the consent of the majority of the people of Northern Ireland voting in a poll held for the purpose of this section in accordance with Schedule 1 to this Act."

. . . This was traditional Unionism as embraced and defended by the four successful unionist leaders Carson, Craigavon, Andrews and Brookeborough, who always said that the price of our liberty was eternal vigilance. Yet now—in a day when everyone knows *that the Union is in dire crisis, under threat, and has been seriously weakened by the Anglo-Irish Agreement, by the Downing Street Declaration, by the Hume/Adams conspiracy, and by Irish-American and European Union interference*—in contrast to these great men we have a Leader of the Ulster Unionist Party who is actually saying that there is no threat to the Union and that the Union cannot be betrayed. Evidently, Mr Molyneaux and the present Official Unionists have not learned the lessons of history.

Carson

Our greatest Leader, Lord Carson, knew that undiminished union with Britain was vital for Ulster's freedom. The fight of Ulster's majority in the days of Lord Carson was consequently the fight for the Union. The struggle to maintain the political, economic and social union with Great Britain was of crucial importance to them. *They knew that the British connection was an essential safeguard for the practice of religion and the freedom to pursue their way of life. They feared the power and influence of the Roman Catholic Church. They did not want citizenship in a State dominated by a religious-political power* which made the rules for the politicians and determined the spiritual standards of belief and the moral standards of conduct for everybody. They refused to be absorbed into a culture which they saw as backward, superstitious and priest-ridden. We have had in the past few weeks the uncovering of the rottenness of the state system of the Irish Republic and its manipulation to cover over priestly crimes for the advantage of the church. When we consider the fate of our co-religionists in the Irish Republic since its inception, 80 percent of whom have disappeared because of discrimination, incompatibility or insecurity, we know that history has confirmed our fathers' worst fears. Ironically, it was the Unionist Party that betrayed the 300,000 Protestants of Southern Ireland in 1921. The British Parliament was at that time overwhelmingly Unionist, and today it is also a Conservative and Unionist Government that is busily engaged in repeating its historical treachery. Lord Carson said:

> "I speak for a good many, for all those who rely on British honour and British justice, who have in giving their best to the service of the state seen themselves now deserted and cast aside without one single line of recollection or recognition in the whole of what you call peace terms in Ireland."

Those words could have been written today. Carson also said: "In my long experience of the Government of the country I have always felt certain that the parties of disorder would in the long run come to the top." We have also seen that happening today. He also said: "I only came into public life because I cared for my fellow loyalists in Ireland. I went all through my public life doing my best for them, and I saw them in the end betrayed, but at all events betrayed under the pretext that certain safeguards were provided. Now I have lived to see every one of those safeguards absolutely set at nought and made useless."

I issue a similar warning today. If we do not resist every step marked out for us by the present British Government, then we will see every so-called safeguard which they mouth set aside at their convenience to further the monstrous act of the final betrayal of the Union. . . .

The present Leader of the official Ulster Unionist Party Mr James Molyneaux, has stated in the midst of this, the worst crisis in Ulster's history since the setting up of the state, that there is no sell-out, that the Union is secure, that the IRA has been conned, and that there is no possibility of betrayal. Let us examine these four assertions.

Firstly, that there is no sell-out. We might well ask what a sell-out is. A sell-out consists of those who should know well the value of what is in their possession and to which they have paid the most wholesome allegiance in words, selling that possession to the enemy. Secondly, Mr Molyneaux asserts that the Union is secure. Two men, Hume and Adams are both the inveterate haters of the Union. They came together and planned a conspiracy against the Union—conspiracy whose details have never been revealed to the people of Northern Ireland. Why? Because men like them love darkness rather than light, because their deeds are evil. From the womb of the Hume/Adams conspiracy came the Downing Street Declaration.

Despite the monstrous blunder of signing the Anglo-Irish Agreement, the British Prime Minister failed to learn the lesson and went even further down the road to a sell-out of the majority community when he and his Southern Irish counterpart, Albert Reynolds, issued a "Joint Declaration" in London on 15th December, 1993, dealing with the future governance of Northern Ireland. *This so-called Downing Street Declaration is a Jesuitical document*, to quote the Jim Molyneaux of that day, but its core is contained in the idea that the Government of the Irish Republic, a foreign State, will work together with the British Government, which declares that it has "no selfish, strategic or economic interest" in Northern Ireland, to achieve "peace, stability and reconciliation established by agreement among all the people to inhabit the island." The agreement would "embrace the totality of relationships." They accept that any such agreement may bring about a united Ireland by consent. Even on a generous interpretation, this represents a significant dilution in the constitutional guarantee hitherto given by the British Government that there would be no change in the status of Northern Ireland without the consent of the majority of its people. If carried out, the policies indicated in *this Declaration will materially weaken the Union and encourage nationalists to believe that their goal of a united Ireland is within easy reach*. The Irish Republic, in effect, achieves an equal say in the governance of the United Kingdom, since the parts thereof are indivisible under the sovereignty of Her Majesty the Queen until the Union is dissolved by the United Kingdom Parliament.

The Downing Street Declaration is in reality the blue-print of the Republic endorsed by Whitehall to destroy Ulster unionists as they have already destroyed Southern Irish unionists. *The Declaration aims through a carefully camouflaged joint partnership of the two Governments, to bring about the sole and sovereign authority of a Dublin Government over us.* The stated objective of the Declaration is to bring about an end to violence. The IRA is to be persuaded to give up the bullet and work through the ballot box. In October, 1994, the IRA declared a so-called ceasefire but no counterfeit ceasefire will convince the people of this Province that the IRA thugs and murderers have had a change of heart. Dublin, like Rome, is the proverbial leopard which cannot change its spots. The Ulster Democratic Unionist Party's predictions have been consistently correct, and events have already proved us right: punishment beatings continue in the no-go areas where the IRA rules, and the IRA has now admitted that it was behind the murder of an innocent Post Office worker in Newry during a robbery which netted over £130,000 for their terrorist activities. Clearly, when the IRA realises that the British Government will be unable to deliver the goal of a united Ireland, it will return to the methods of coercion that it knows best—bombing and murder.

The Downing Street Declaration, like its forerunner the Anglo-Irish Agreement, had the aim of betraying the Ulster people, bribing the IRA and appeasing the Republican enemy. It was a total breach of the promises that Major had made on 10th December, 1993, that no Government he led would compromise the constitutional position of Northern Ireland, negotiate or bargain with terrorists, or derogate from United Kingdom sovereignty in the Province. . . .

One has only to look around to note the betrayals of a Prime Minister who Mr Molyneaux said never told a lie.

- One—The Prime Minister said that the IRA must repudiate and renounce violence. That is exactly what the IRA has not done. The Prime Minister said that there must be a complete cessation of violence. That **complete cessation of violence has not taken place**, and during the so-called three month period of the ceasefire there has been a whole tide of vicious violence, culminating in the self-confessed murder by the IRA of Mr Kerr in Newry and the stealing of £130,000 from the Royal Mail.
- Two—Mr Major maintained that the word "permanent" must be in the IRA's declaration. In fact an ultimatum of a few hours was given by the Secretary of State to get the word "permanent" into the declaration. Once again Mr Major went back on that principle.
- Three—Mr Major said there could be no clarification whatsoever of the Downing Street Declaration. Then he took large pages in newspapers to clarify the Downing Street Declaration, and then he got the Secretary of State to write a love letter of over 20 pages to Gerry Adams in order that Adams might have the Downing Street Declaration clarified.
- Four—Mr Major maintained that the South of Ireland would have no say in the internal settlement in Northern Ireland. Yet the whole force of his negotiations with Dublin after the Downing Street Declaration, have been along the lines of an internal settlement in Northern Ireland agreeable to the Irish Republic. He is the first Prime Minister who has handed over any part of the United Kingdom to be governed jointly by himself and the Prime Minister of a traditional enemy country, a country claiming sovereignty over Northern Ireland. Mr Major promised he would come to grips with getting rid of the territorial claims of Articles 2 and 3. Dublin has made it clear that as far as Article 2 is concerned it will never be removed from the Republic's Constitution. Evidently Mr Major has given up the ghost on this one as well. How can anyone tell us that the Union cannot be betrayed when we have only to open our eyes and see betrayal on every hand? . . .

The Issue of Consent

For the people of Northern Ireland, the principle of consent freely given must prevail over the bullet, in the way in which they are to be governed in future. There can be neither compromise with terrorist minority pressure nor external interference by a foreign state in their internal governance. . . .

The ballot box, not the bullet, must prevail in Northern Ireland. The freely expressed democratic will of the people of the Province must be respected and implemented. By the same token, *a commitment to the principle of democratic consent rules out not only any compromise with the terrorists of IRA/Sinn Féin, but also any imposed solution.* Neither will work. The former is morally unthinkable; the latter, already tested in principle through direct rule and the Anglo Irish Diktat, has had nothing but disastrous consequences. Both conceptions breach the right of the people of the Province to decide their own future, including how they are to be governed, democratically without pressure or interference.

For the avoidance of any doubt we call on Mr Major to clarify unambiguously that Her Majesty's Government will: (a) accept and abide by the verdict of a majority in a referendum; (b) accept that a referendum of the people of Northern Ireland alone will determine any change; (c) undertake to implement a referendum prior to implementing any change; (d) commit itself to holding a referendum on change impacting upon Northern Ireland in all circumstances and for all time; (e) seek Parliamentary endorsement for this principle of consent. . . .

Let me speak a final word. Are we, the sons and daughters of Ulster become so craven as to allow our ancient foes to triumph over us? Are we the offspring of the defenders of Londonderry and the descendents [sic] of the men of the Boyne given to turning back in the day of battle? Are we going to surrender to a State so blatantly priest-ridden and core rotten as to be the butt of all right thing [sic] peoples throughout the world? The last few days have demonstrated the stinking rottenness of the corpse of body politic in Dublin. *Are we going to bow our necks and agree to a partnership with the IRA men of blood who have slain our loved ones, destroyed our country, burned our churches, tortured our people and demand now that we should become slaves in a country fit only for Nuns men and Monks women to live in?*

Are we going to permit those who wear the garments of Unionism to lead us by the nose to the noose which our false friends in London have prepared for us?

Are we going to suffer ourselves to become beggars at the door of the American Whitewashed House presenting our bowls for the mess of American grits?

Are we like abject slaves to Salam the new United States overlord sent to us by the Whitewater crook? Are we going to allow minor Majors or major Minors to take us for a ride to the paedophile priests?

Rouse you, men and women of Ulster. You are free born. Refuse the chains prepared for you by treacherous unionists and their ilk.

Let Dublin know that there still be those who must not, shall not, will not, and cannot bow to these traitors who tread the smoke-filled rooms of Whitehall, nor to those enemies the offspring of the Vatican who walk the corrupted corridors of power in Dublin, in Europe and in Washington.

In the propaganda war we must excel answering the lies with truth and smoking out from their lairs the media skunks and cleansing their putrid odour from the earth.

Ulster men and women we mean business, real business. To the task of saving this Province we have put our hand. By God's help we will win or die in the attempt.

God Save Ulster.

22. David Ervine Speech to the Progressive Unionist Conference, 1997

David Ervine was a member of the Ulster Volunteer Force (UVF) who served six years in prison for possessing explosives. On leaving prison in 1980 he devoted himself to the PUP, the political arm of the UVF, and after the paramilitary ceasefire in 1994 he became one of its chief spokespersons.

Source: Progressive Unionist Party, accessed 30 April 2019, https://www.pup-ni.org.uk/statements/speech/de.htm (site discontinued).

On entering our twentieth year in Northern Ireland politics the Progressive Unionist Party reaffirms that it is wholly and unequivocally committed to achieving it's [sic] *political* goals exclusively through *democratic and peaceful means.*

There is no room whatever in our philosophy for violence of any description from whatever source, for whatever reason.

The greater number of people in Northern Ireland desire the continuance of the Union with Britain which has been proven time and time again in democratic Elections. This palpable fact is recognised by both British and Irish governments, plus the whole of political and corporate America as well as the other World democracies. So be it.

Let no one be under any illusion that, in their hearts, the Provos, too, accept this reality but are having the greatest difficulty coming to terms with it and the fact that tile [sic] Unionist population are the real British presence in Northern Ireland. . . .

Political shenanigans and distractions by political parties contributed to semi-stagnation whereas had all-Party talks taken place evasiveness and intransigence would have been placed in perspective and dealt with in a methodical and substantial way in a first step towards the reformation of our society.

Reforms are needed and are long overdue but we need the power to enable us to make the necessary change. A whole plethora of communal, social and economic ills are going unaddressed because of political instability and as a result it is the deprived who are being further disadvantaged. . . .

We, in our Party, know only too well what needs to be done in Northern Ireland in political terms and we will play a full role in bringing about a society where everyone has a voice and an input commensurate with their political mandate. Our society needs full-time politicians. Politics is a profession and requires whatever skills, time and commitment it takes to get the job done well. Most politicians in Northern Ireland have other professions and, however willing, it is difficult to see how they can divide themselves adequately in one profession and yet fully represent a constituency politically. The P.U.P. Political and Advisory Centres are open all day for five-and-a-half days of the week . . . every week!

We expect no favours and it is certain we shall receive none. We do not over-estimate our importance, but we are important to the process and so, too, is Sinn Féin if the IRA will permit them to enter into dialogue by declaring a credible and lasting cease-fire. *We say now that there has to be a reinstatement of the IRA cease-fire because they cannot be included in negotiations without one being in place.* Democracy cannot wait and for them, it is "make your mind up time." They must join now or get left behind.

In a civilised society, frustration with the lack of political progress does not warrant murder, mortars and mayhem.

Further isolation of Sinn Féin has been the only consequence of the IRA's illogical actions and the question is seriously being begged "has the methods of the Provos become more sacred than the Cause"?

Such an overwhelming and over-powering level of opposition to violence cannot be ignored by any group or party seeking political ratification at the polls. They cannot purport to run on a "peace ticket" this time around.

The Northern Ireland political idealistic epicentre is not based in some time-warped version of Irish Republicanism but in the reality of what is acceptable, possible and applicable in these Islands.

It has been mostly working-class people who have

borne the brunt of the violence over these past twenty-five years, and they are sick and tired of political sabre-rattling and mischievousness from whatever quarter.

There can never, ever, be a return to the awful political and social abuses of the past and Stormont as we knew it is dead and gone, never to be resurrected. Granted there are those political dinosaurs who would opt for the "good old" sectarian and strata system of the past where everybody knew their place and forelock touching was the norm. We have had enough of that obnoxious trio . . . bigotry, sectarianism and hypocrisy.

We would oppose as vehemently and strenuously as anyone else a return to such a divisive and partisan system of government.

The Progressives are not airy-fairy idealists but we do have imagination and we know what can happen when people sit down to reason together for the benefit of every section of our divided society.

In the last year's Forum elections we received a credible 26,082 votes which we believe is just a stepping-stone to bigger things. We have taken the most difficult step of all, the first step in playing a fuller role in the political life of our Country and we clearly realise the enormity of all that this entails. We will give the people, all the people, a real alternative to the politicians and the politics of the past which have so ill-served our divided community. We have made a positive impact on the political scene especially amongst the younger element in our society, who for a variety of reasons are more politically perceptive and more willing to embrace change. *We all know that our society must change* and so long as we, together, are the masters of change we can stride confidently into the future sure in the knowledge that at long last through courage, compromise and vision we can attain that which has eluded us for so long and to finally end the waking nightmare of past decades ultimately resulting in this society being at peace with itself and with its neighbours.

23. David Trimble Speech at the Annual General Meeting of the Ulster Unionist Council, 1996

David Trimble was elected as to Parliament as a member of the Ulster Unionist Party in 1990 and then selected as leader of the UUP in 1995. He gave this speech on 23 March 1996.

Source: "Irish Peace Process: List of Source Documents," CAIN, accessed 30 April 2019, https://cain.ulster.ac.uk/events/peace/docs/dt23396.htm.

The Canary Wharf bomb clearly and conclusively proves that there is no prospect of the republican movement becoming committed to exclusively peaceful means.

The duty of government is clear. But the British and Irish Governments have shirked that duty. Instead of making terrorists amenable to the law, they have responded to their agenda asking in return only for a "credible ceasefire."

The concept of a credible ceasefire is now a contradiction in terms.

Instead of a resolute defence of the community we have the pathetic and degrading sight of democratically elected politicians pleading with terrorists. . . .

Mr Bruton, If you seriously want peace, as you say you do, there is one simple way of getting it. Close down the IRA. Do not tell us you cannot. Your predecessors did exactly that three times!

And Mr Clinton, if you want to help, remember how you have just arranged to supply Israel with 100 million dollars worth of anti-terrorist technological assistance. Why don't you consider supplying the Irish Republic with the intelligence equipment it so obviously lacks. And if from your resources you can supply Dublin with the odd backbone it would help!

And Mr Major, if you seriously want peace and Mr Bruton seems a wee bit uncertain, then you have a fairly simple way of encouraging him to your way of thinking. End the common travel area. Control the land and sea frontier. Once the Dublin government realises that it can no longer export bombs along with its social problems to England, it will become as helpful as a Tory backbencher in search of a knighthood.

PEACE AND DEMOCRACY

Our fundamental concerns are peace and democracy. In the language of the peace process they are called consent and decommissioning.

DECOMMISSIONING

The need to decommission derives from the democratic principle. Parties should come to the table on the basis of their votes not their guns. We remember President Clinton's words in West Belfast, "There is no place for guns at the table of democracy." Those words echoed John Hume's statement that there should be no guns at the table, under the table or outside the door. The time will come, John, for you to honour those words just as the paramilitaries will have to make and honour a commitment to the Mitchell Report. As the President said at a press conference in the White House last Friday, before the St Patrick's day reception, "The decommissioning issue has to be addressed and has to be resolved. Senator Mitchell did a very good job, I thought, of dealing with that whole issue." . . .

The Government statement of 28 February only makes sense on the basis of giving Sinn Féin/IRA a last chance and then of going on without them if they do not take it. In this the present plans differ from the last 18 months. Then the refusal of Sinn Féin to commit itself to peace blocked talks and prevented all the other parties from proceeding. Now their refusal should only veto themselves and those who prefer their company. We proceed on that basis. The alternative would be appeasement and surrender to which we will not be a party.

CONSENT

Consent simply means that it is for the people of Northern Ireland as a whole, and for them alone, to determine their constitutional destiny.

Elections are obviously the embodiment of that democratic principle. Any talks must be clearly embedded within the democratic process. But elections do more than that. They involve the people of Northern Ireland as participants in determining their future rather than passive spectators awaiting the judgement of others. They provide a public forum through which public opinion, especially outside Northern Ireland can be educated, and where issues can be ventilated and the acceptability of possible outcomes tested. . . .

Sooner or later the SDLP like others will have to come to terms with the fact that it is for the people of Northern Ireland to determine to which state they belong.

Some say this reflects an old-fashioned view of sovereignty and that the issue of which state you belong to can be blurred or fudged. That is wrong. Sovereignty today is essential to protect the democratic principle. The question is, to whom do you pay your taxes? Who takes decisions concerning your rights and your future? Are those persons elected by you? Do they account to you and can you turn them out if they make the wrong decisions?

These are the most fundamental questions that can be asked about the political arrangements of any society. These questions can be answered in a United Kingdom context or a Republic of Ireland context: but they cannot be answered democratically in a condominium or any form of joint British/Irish constitutional fudge.

REPAIRING THE DAMAGE

It is equally clear that these questions cannot be answered satisfactorily in Ulster today. It is only with respect to those decisions that are truly made on a United Kingdom basis, that is decisions that apply equally throughout the Kingdom, that we can say that decision makers are accountable to us as part of the United Kingdom electorate. For decisions taken on a purely Northern Ireland basis, or worse decisions taken as a result of the Anglo-Irish process, are not accountable to us.

That reminds us of one of our objectives in these talks. We cannot be satisfied with the status quo. That status quo demeans our democratic rights. It makes us second class citizens on a broad range of issues. It is for that reason that we want to replace the Diktat and repair the damage to the Union.

That repair job can and should start at both ends, building up accountable democracy here through strengthened local government and a new Assembly, and building at the Westminster end through democratic procedures for Northern Ireland business. . . .

We want an Assembly where there is accountability to all the people of Northern Ireland and all of our people can, if they wish, participate meaningfully.

MAJORITARIANISM?

When we speak of this democratic deficit there are those who accuse us of longing for majority rule. This is unfair. Of course in any democracy when choices have to be made then, if all else fails, the greater number, however it might be composed, must prevail. Thus it was on the issue of whether Quebec would remain a part of Canada. That question was determined by a margin of 50.6 percent to 49.4 percent. Thus it was in the Republic of Ireland on the issue of divorce. That question was settled by a margin of 50.3 percent to 49.7 percent.

But if simple majorities are a necessary condition of democracy they are not always a sufficient condition. It is clearly desirable to have as broad a basis of support as it is possible to achieve. That is why we want every reasonable assurance of fairness. Thus we propose an Assembly that will operate on the basis of proportionality, where the elections, the committees, and the chairmanships will be proportional. Every party will be able to participate at every level in proportion to their votes.

RIGHTS PROTECTED

We have developed comprehensive proposals for the protection of the human and civil rights. This involves important new ground. Unlike political institutions the protection of rights can easily transcend frontiers. This has long been the case with regard to the rights protected by the European Convention. But in the last decade European states have extended protection to ethnic and national minorities. The Europe I refer to is not the 15 states of the European Community but the 50 plus states of the real Europe, many of whom do have serious minority problems.

These states acting through the Organisation for Security and Co-operation in Europe have developed a code of practice relating to national minorities. It involves the recognition of existing frontiers, respecting the rights of the state, and guaranteeing the rights of minorities. It is contained in the Charter of Paris (1990) and other agreements. A Commissioner for National Minorities has been established. The Moscow Mechanism has been created whereby a state may address questions to another state where it believes minorities are being treated unfairly. Last year the Council of Europe concluded a Convention on the Rights of Minorities. This is how the rest of Europe has tackled the substance of the matters referred to under the phrase parity of esteem. Nationalists would do well to follow these examples.

If the Republic wants to act as a guarantor of the rights of northern nationalists, then it no longer needs the Anglo-Irish agreement. It can follow these European precedents. If it clings to the Diktat then it is open to the suspicion that it wants to extend its power within Ulster and take another step towards realizing articles 2 and 3 and bringing about a United Ireland. The elections, however, will show that there is no consent for constitutional change. They will be a barrier to Dublin's ambitions. They will show the people of Ulster yearn for peace and democracy.

We will go forward seeking to realize those goals. We will defend the democratic principle. We will strive to fill the democratic deficit and create worthwhile local representative bodies on which all men of goodwill can agree and work to create the future we know is possible.

SECTION F. NATIONALIST POLITICAL DOCUMENTS OF THE 1990S

24. Excerpt from John Hume's Leader's Address to the Social Democratic and Labour Party 25th Annual Conference, 1995

John Hume served as a member of the European Parliament beginning in 1979 and of the British beginning in 1983. He became active in the civil rights movement in Derry/Londonderry in the 1960s and then helped form the Social Democratic and Labour Party (SDLP) in 1970, rising to be its leader in 1979. Although Nationalist, the SDLP and Hume focused on improving Catholics' political and economic position in Northern Ireland instead of reunifying with the Irish Republic, and they regularly condemned violence. Secret talks between John Hume and Gerry Adams helped to form the background to the nationalists' approach to the Irish and British governments for talks in the early 1990s.

Source: "John Hume," CAIN, accessed 25 April 2019, https://cain.ulster.ac.uk/john_hume/docs/Hume_1995-11-18_address.pdf.

The SDLP has consistently pointed out that the territorial mentality of traditional nationalism must go. That it is the people of Ireland who are divided and not the territory and they can only be brought together by agreement and by no form of coercion. That is now accepted by the entire nationalist tradition and our major challenge now when at the table will be to have the flexibility of ideas to reach a new agreement with the unionist people. The physical border in Ireland with the removal of checkpoints is now gone as are all borders within the European Union permitting free movement of people, goods and services. The real border remains in the hearts and minds of people and it cannot be removed by one instant package or in a short period of time. It will require a healing process and the creation of agreed institutions which will allow us to work together in our common interests and let the healing process begin. . . .

Moving our minds and hearts will always bring more progress and stability that [*sic*] making maps or waving flags. While identity is very important our most fundamental feature is our humanity. We are born human beings before we are anything else. No two human beings are the same even if they have the same name, nationality, ethnicity, gender, class, colour or creed. Difference is the essence of creation. Acceptance and accommodation of difference must also be the essence of creative politics.

25. Excerpts from John Hume's *A New Ireland*

Source: John Hume, *A New Ireland: Politics, Peace, and Reconciliation* (Boulder, CO: Roberts Rinehart, 1996), 48–52, 95–96.

When a society produces alienation in the individual, when it cannot provide for the equality and the differences of its citizens, "when the social system does not build security but induces peril," that society must be reshaped and transformed through new institutions which accommodate diversity and promote the best basis for reconciliation.

This is the only way forward in Northern Ireland. Let me demonstrate this by considering briefly the alternatives offered. There is the traditional Unionist approach, of seeking the exclusive exercise of political power in Northern Ireland for themselves, of ignoring the existence of a community comprising forty per cent of the area's population, who have a different identity and a different aspiration. They hark back to the past and speak of the future only with fear and foreboding. . . .

The conflict reflects a sad condition, a siege mentality rooted in insecurity in prejudice, in fear of domination by a Catholic majority in Ireland, so-called "Rome Rule," a bitter play on "Home Rule" which was a policy of self-autonomy rejected by Unionists in 1912. Even if, in the light of history and of the violent campaign of the IRA, some of these fears are understandable, they are groundless. *There can be no solution to our problem which seeks to destroy or to crush the Protestant heritage in Ireland. It would be unthinkable. Accommodation of difference is the only basis for peace and stability in our divided society.* I have always avowed that simple truth.

Then there is the other alternative, that of the Provisional IRA and Sinn Féin. For twenty-five years we in the SDLP have opposed the IRA. We have pointed out in critical statements of their actions that the IRA has bombed factories while Sinn Féin shouts about unemployment; that the IRA shot a teacher in a classroom, killed school bus drivers, killed people on campuses, and then Sinn Féin lectures us about education; that the IRA maimed and injured, and carried out attacks in hospital precincts while Sinn Féin talks about protecting the Health Service. The real strategy and objectives were clear. In our view, the IRA created as much discontent and deprivation as possible, including unemployment. Then Sinn Féin was trying to feed off the people's discontent.

My party the SDLP, born out of the civil rights movement, long ago rejected these two purported alternatives which in fact offer no hope for the future. Like Martin Luther King, we had a dream; like Theobald Wolfe Tone, the father of Irish republicanism, *our vision has been "to substitute for the denomination of Catholic, Protestant and Dissenter the common name of Irishman." Our chosen strategy encompassed reform, reconciliation, and reunification* along a path of steady progress, continually narrowing the gap between the reality and the dream, using the political means of dialogue, persuasion, negotiation, accommodation, compromise. *Violence can never heal the deep wounds that divide a people. Only a healing process can in time end the division in Ireland.* And it will take time.

Our analysis is that the *first necessary step in that healing process is the creation of total equality of treatment of all the citizens of Northern Ireland, Nationalists and Unionists alike, from basic civil rights to full expression of their identity.* . . .

Thus, the process of bringing about practical recognition and respect for equality between the two identities and communities remains to be completed. . . .

On the basis of that equality, because *reconciliation can only be based on equality*, comes the process of reconciliation, the second element in my party's long-term programme, the breaking down of barriers between the different sections of our people. No one can underestimate the difficulty of that task. It will take time, but it is a task that involves everyone and that will lead, coming to the third major element, to the only Irish unity that really matters, the only unity that all pre-partition leaders spoke of, a unity that respects diversity and legitimises differences. That is a process and objective that no one need fear because everyone must be part of the building process. . . .

The process of reform and reconciliation can best be tackled through a framework corresponding to the framework of the problem and thus, through the British-Irish framework, through an approach that deals with the three major dimensions of the problem—relations between the two communities in Northern Ireland, relations between both parties, the Nationalist and Unionist traditions in Ireland as a whole, and relations between Ireland and Britain. . . .

My party wishes to demonstrate the potential of democratic politics and of the philosophy of non-violence to make progress toward the resolution of what is perhaps one of the more intractable political problems in the world today. I believe that these same principles are applicable in the field of international relations. When we are dealing with human conflict whether in a divided community, a divided country or a divided globe, it is the building of mutual trust and not mutual fear that will solve the problem of conflict—not just in Ireland, but around the world—because we know that human beings are no different wherever they live. . . .

England saw Ireland as the back door for her European enemies and moved into Ireland to defend her own interests, with all the serious consequences for the Irish people.

All that has now changed and *both Ireland and Britain are members of the European Union*. . . .

It is quite clear, therefore, that no one could argue that Britain is in Ireland today defending either military or economic interests. Issues like independence and sovereignty, issues at the heart of the British-Irish quarrel, have changed their meaning in the new Europe because *we now have interdependence and shared sovereignty*. . . .

If bitter enemies like France and Germany can build new relationships, can we not do the same?

26. Gerry Adams Speech to the Sinn Féin Ard Fheis (Annual Party Conference), 1994

Gerry Adams, president of Sinn Féin since 1983, has long been reputed to be a senior figure in the IRA, a charge he denies. He was key in helping the party develop a more active political strategy after the hunger strikes of 1981 and was elected MP on an abstentionist basis (that is, Sinn Féin ran candidates but refused to take their seats in Parliament as a denial of British authority over Northern Ireland) from 1983 to 1992. Secret talks between Adams and John Hume helped to form the background to the nationalists' approach to the Irish and British governments for talks in the early 1990s.

Source: "Key Issues," CAIN, accessed 28 July 2019, https://cain.ulster.ac.uk/issues/politics/docs/sf/ga_1994.htm.

Welcome to you all. I extend greetings and solidarity to the families of republican prisoners and to the prisoners themselves here in Ireland, in Britain and throughout the world.

We are meeting here this weekend at an historic juncture in the struggle for Irish democracy. The events of this past six months have moved at a breathtaking pace as change unfolded rapidly. At the centre of the whirlpool of developments is the prize of peace, much sought after by all sensible people in both these islands. For the last quarter of a century, the political landscape has been frozen over—those with real power to thaw out the situation seemed to be in a permanent state of paralysis.

But the ice is beginning to thaw and much has been done in the last six months to create the climate wherein a real debate, open-ended and inclusive of everyone, can take place. But a lot more needs to be done before certainty of purpose can replace the atmosphere of suspicion and doubt on all sides. . . .

This Ard Fheis takes no satisfaction from any death. Sinn Féin represents a section of the Irish people who have had to attend too many funerals and who have had to endure too much suffering. Our solidarity with other victims is founded in our own experience and in our own grief. Our expressions of sympathy are genuine and heartfelt.

I want to deal now with the relentless campaign of the loyalist death squads. Since 1988, when the South African weapons were brought into Ireland by Brian Nelson, with the knowledge and approval of British intelligence, 198 people have been killed by loyalist death squads, 176 of these were sectarian killings. These bereaved families receive a minimum of media attention. *Nationalists in the North are murdered, buried and their families are left to grieve in isolation. Nationalists feel that in death, as in life, they are treated as second-class citizens.* Attacks by loyalist death squads, even when they are against civilians at funerals, or in bookmakers shops, or against individual Catholics, or the families of Sinn Féin activists or SDLP members, are not as indiscriminate as they are often portrayed.

The objectives are specific and clear. One of these is to terrorise. For this reason, as in similar situations in South Africa, Palestine or parts of Central America, where minorities resist democratic change, noninvolved civilians, families, women and children are the premeditated targets. The aim is to terrorise as many people as possible and to make all perceived opponents feel that they could be the next victim.

The weapons and propaganda of loyalism today may be modern. The intent and the reason for its existence and behaviour and its sponsors and backers remain as before.

It is important also to understand that while the

loyalists have their own agenda, their attacks also fit into British counterinsurgency strategy. This is why there has always been collusion, both at an official and unofficial or personal level. Examples of this collusion are many, from the Dublin and Monaghan bombings to the Brian Nelson affair. They predate this phase of the conflict. Attempts by the British to distance themselves from, or to deny involvement in loyalist terrorism are totally at variance with the historical and contemporary record. Collusion between elements of the British military and intelligence community and the loyalist death squads is a fact of life and death in Ireland.

We are told that loyalist actions are reactive. Yet the first major post-war riot in Belfast in 1964 was incited by Ian Paisley. The first murders of Catholics —just because they were Catholics—in this period occurred on the Shankill Road in Belfast in 1966, where the first RUC man was killed some years later. Loyalist violence was used against the early Civil Rights Movement and the first bomb explosion was the work of loyalists. The activities of loyalist death squads have been most intense during suspensions of IRA activity in 1972 and 1975—a complete contradiction of assertions that loyalist violence is simply reactive to the IRA.

Loyalist extreme reaction occurs when there are signs of political progress, of the croppies getting up off our knees. This is the reality of the situation. It has been so for a very long time now and it will continue to be so while one section of our people believe that their selfish interests can only be advanced by the repression of another section. From its inception, the Six-County statelet was stamped with the mark of sectarian violence and its unionist leaders were, and are, all politically on the extreme right. That statelet is still the greatest political monument to religious sectarianism in Ireland and its unionist politicians feel no shame in appealing to the most backward sort of religious prejudices when it suits them.

Yet they are supported, and have been supported, by the British ruling class. Of course, British politicians and others would be anxious to deplore bigotry and indeed some may be genuinely embarrassed by some cruder aspects of unionist sectarianism. They like to disassociate themselves from these expressions of their principles but they know that this is a fundamental ingredient of grass-roots unionism, and not the sole prerogative of Paisley and his bellowing bigotry, or in Jim Molyneaux's tight-lipped service to reaction. They also know, though they may not like to admit it, *that the Anglo/Irish problem is compounded by the support which the British government gives to unionism and the inability, therefore, of unionists to come to a democratic accommodation with the rest of the Irish people.*

The British government supports the union and the unionist minority in our country. This is the nub of the problem between Ireland and Britain.

Loyalism is part of the British way of life in Ireland. It, like unionism, is a child of the British connection. Its extremists will be redundant when that connection is severed and when the Protestant section of our community can shake off the shackles of unionism. The development of democracy in Ireland is smothered by the union.

Democracy Demands Irish Self-Determination.

In the struggle to achieve this and in the face of such terrorism, republicans must always be aware of the justness of our cause and the intentions of our opponents. Our task is to frustrate these intentions, not to serve them. We must never sink to their level. The loyalist death squads, and their masters, are yesterday's people. We must aim towards tomorrow, not yesterday. We can take succour from the truth that their peculiar and utterly irrational blind bigotry cannot survive for long when the political circumstances which breed it and which nourish it are removed. Any movement towards a peaceful settlement of the conflict must therefore aim to remove these circumstances. That is our firm intention. It must also become the intention of the British government.

First and most reasonably—and immediately on the opening of any serious talks—that government must deliver a convincing indication of their sincere intent to pursue an attainable formula for a lasting peace. That means them withdrawing political support from the unionists.

The unionists must be relieved, by those who have supplied them for so long, of the delusions that have sustained them. *The unionists must be told plainly that, contrary to their illogical belief, the Six-County area does not belong to them. It belongs to all our people equally, irrespective of falsely created majorities and minorities.*

Protestants need to be encouraged to recognise that they share a common history with their Catholic fellow-countrymen and women. . . .

I want once again to assure northern Protestants, that the republican demand for British withdrawal is not aimed at them. It is directed solely at the British government's control in Ireland. It is a demand that the people of Ireland, and that includes the essential contribution and participation of northern Protestants, be allowed to control our own destiny and shape a society which is pluralist and reflective of the diversity of all our people. . . .

The Protestants of the North have been cheated for long enough. They have been cheated by being ensnared into that sectarian trap prepared for them by British imperial administrations. They can be released from that trap if peace negotiations are allowed to follow a realistic course.

Peace Process

The republican struggle has often been described as ineffective, out-of-date or counterproductive. Such claims are no more than the wishful thinking of our political opponents echoing the political propaganda of our enemies.

Twenty-five years ago the nationalists of the North were an impotent, suppressed and largely apathetic section of the Irish people, locked against our will, without our consent, into a vicious sectarian state. The British government, as much as the bigotry of unionism, was responsible for this, and successive Dublin governments allowed this unjust situation to continue. There is no avoiding the fact that it was the policies, or lack of policies, of both governments, respectively, which contributed so much to the terrible tragedy with which we are now living. In December, the leaders of these two governments were moved to address republicans directly through the Downing Street Declaration.

This effort to address republicans directly is a fundamental shift in policy and in contrast to strategies which aimed to ignore republicanism as part of a policy of marginalising and isolating us. Like all other initiatives, this one marks the failure of every strategy which preceded it. It is also specifically, a direct response to the developing, and increasingly effective, peace strategy which Sinn Féin publicly launched almost seven years ago and which we are totally committed to bringing to a positive conclusion. . . .

We have reasonably and rationally held up the democratic and universally accepted principle of national self-determination as the route through which that can come about. We have argued that both the London and Dublin governments should adopt this as their policy objective, to be achieved within an agreed timescale—in other words, as part of a process. Again, both reasonably and rationally, we have argued that this be accomplished in consultation with all the parties involved, and the consent of the unionists must be actively sought during this process, a process during which national reconciliation can begin, a process of negotiations culminating in a negotiated settlement.

In all of this we have correctly identified the British government as the major player. They have the power and responsibility to move things on. Their policy in Ireland casts them, either in the role of keepers of the status quo or as key persuaders in forward movement towards a lasting peace, founded on democratic principles. We have also correctly recognised that a united Irish nationalist/republican voice in support of such an end and a process for its achievement, as being a potent political force, not just in Ireland itself but in Britain and internationally.

The sub-theme of that, of course, is that Irish republicans, by ourselves, simply do not possess the political strength to bring about these aims. While that situation obtains, it must continue to influence the political and strategic thinking of Irish republicans. However, we do possess the ability to create conditions which can move the situation towards these aims and we have the power to prevent another settlement on British government terms, which would subvert Irish national and democratic rights.

We fully accept and acknowledge that there is no quick-fix to this. A peace process has been set in train. Our immediate and ongoing task is to move this process onwards. With the evolution of policy and in particular, our thinking on Sinn Féin's peace strategy, we aimed to provide a broad strategy, a momentum and a framework which took on board both the political reality confronting us and our desire, despite the many difficulties this represented, to advance our peace strategy. It is in this context that we should examine the potential of any proposal put before us. . . .

The Irish Peace Initiative
My talks with SDLP leader John Hume have been the most significant element in the peace process so far. As is now well known, we reached agreement on a process based upon a set of principles, containing the political dynamic which could create the conditions for a lasting peace and a total demilitarisation of the situation. This was dependent on the adoption of these proposals by the two governments and a positive attitude from the leadership of the IRA.

John Hume has been subjected to a lot of vilification for engaging in this dialogue and initiative. It has been a risky enterprise for him. I am sure republicans, for totally different reasons, have also been mindful of the risks from our perspective and I have no doubt that there must have been (maybe there remain), and there may be again, occasions when some of you will be justifiably nervous about what is, or is not, going on. After all, Sinn Féin and the SDLP remain locked in electoral, as well as ideological battles and we have lots of reasons from our respective experiences to be distrustful of each other. John Hume and I have never attempted to disguise the political differences between our parties. What we have attempted to do is to put the cause of peace and a negotiated settlement before narrower party political considerations.

My republican analysis is, of course, not identical with that of Mr Hume on all the issues of the day. For example, I would not agree with his views on the out-of-datedness of the nation state, which we regard as the basis of democracy. Also, we do not believe that we are living in a post-nationalist world. But we are at one with him to holding that "an internal settlement is not a solution" and "that the Irish people as a whole have the right to national self-determination," and "it is the search for that agreement and the means of achieving it on which we will be concentrating."

It is obvious that the Irish Peace Initiative—and particularly the agreement between Mr Hume and myself— acted as a major catalyst, not only on Irish nationalist opinion, North and South, but also on focusing the two governments on the issue of peace in Ireland in an unprecedented manner. . . .

However, the serious flaw in the document [the Downing Street Declaration] is that having declared that the Irish are entitled to exercise the right to self-determination without external interference, they then proceed, or so it seems to me, to interfere. This is at odds with the meaning of self-determination. A nation cannot have a half right, or a quarter right to self-determination. There can be no justification for trying to instruct the people whose right to self-determination you have just conceded, how they are to use it. . . .

It is worth repeating again that how Irish national self-determination is exercised is a matter for the Irish people to decide. It is not the business of the British. In my discussions with John Hume we accepted "that the Irish people as a whole have a right to self-determination." We went on to say, "this is a view shared by a majority of people on this island, though not by all its people. The exercise of self-determination is a matter for agreement between the people of Ireland. It is the search for that agreement, and the means of achieving it on which we will be concentrating. We are mindful that not all the people of Ireland share that view or agree on how to give meaningful expression to it. Indeed we cannot disguise the different views held by our different parties. As leaders of our respective parties, we have told each other that we see the task of reaching agreement on a peaceful and democratic accord for all on this island as our primary challenge."

This remains the challenge. It is a challenge for all of the Irish people without external interference. Having addressed the issue, the British should now move to permit the Irish people to take up that challenge and they should seek to persuade the unionists that their future lies in that context.

There are other issues of concern which many people have brought to my attention. For example, northern nationalists are not even explicitly mentioned in the declaration, though there are numerous references to the unionists. John Major tells us why this is so saying: "I have gone to great trouble to ensure that the constitutional guarantee is firmly enshrined in the Joint Declaration, so that there can be no doubt that those people who care about the union—and we are primarily concerned about the people in Northern Ireland who care about the union—shall have it within their own hands, with the full support of the government, to remain within the union for so long as that is their wish."

Are Nationalists Invisible, Mr Major?

Yet at the heart of northern nationalist concerns are fears about loyalist violence and unionist bigotry, the intimidation of nationalist communities by the British army and the social deprivation and job discrimination. Also, there is the denial of full and equal recognition of Irish cultural rights within the Six Counties....

On the positive side, Major says that Britain has no longer any "selfish, economic or strategic interest" in staying in Ireland. In a general sense that may be true as a result of the ending of the Cold War and the unlikelihood of a war in the North Atlantic. He fails to say that they have no political interest. Indeed he asserts that his interest is to uphold the union....

The Downing Street Declaration marks a stage in the slow and painful process of England's disengagement from her first and last colony, Ireland. It may be a small step, as was the Hillsborough Agreement of 1985, which—leaving aside justifiable republican criticisms—gave Dublin, for the first time, a "foot inside the door" in the Six Counties. That door, which is now slightly ajar as a result of the struggle and sacrifices of the past 25 years, culminating in the advances made possible by the Irish peace initiative, needs now to be pushed wide open to let the clean, fresh and invigorating air of Irish democracy blow through the politically stagnant atmosphere of the Six-County prison house which so many of us have to endure and which we are so anxious to get rid of....

The British Government, the IRA and Sinn Féin

Last year, in response to questions from journalists, I made it clear that if a peace package is produced, that I am quite prepared to take this to the IRA. I am, of course, seeking a package which would allow me to make definitive proposals to the IRA in relation to the future conduct of its campaign. It would then be up to the IRA to decide. I am quite confident that the IRA would respond positively to a package containing the principles, process and dynamic which were presented to the British government as a result of the initiative undertaken by John Hume and I.

To the best of my knowledge the IRA's door remains open and the IRA leadership has outlined its positive attitude to these proposals in a series of public statements. Why does London say no? If a formula of words was all that was required one has to presume that we would have had peace two decades ago. The reality is, of course, quite different. There is a conflict. We, therefore, need a programme to end it. The governments cannot argue that they have a basis for peace unless they can produce and explain what it is.

The Dublin government has been concerned to do this but both governments need to do this because while Sinn Féin remains committed to building a real peace process, as I have said many times before, we cannot do so without the cooperation of the British government. Given the historic and current stance of that government this will not be an easy task. As I have said before I will not mislead the IRA. Neither will I mislead others about the IRA.

The British are in no doubt, I am sure, about the capacity and commitment of the IRA. If this is the case then it appears to me that the utterances of British ministers, including Mr Major, especially since 15 December, are deliberately provocative. They persist with their stubborn refusal to recognise the validity of Sinn Féin's electoral mandate. They refuse to admit that our call for clarification is a reasonable one. Yet all other parties receive clarification on request and there appears to be no end to clarifications of a provocative and negative nature, about "decontamination" periods, about "no amnesty for political prisoners," about an "IRA surrender of weapons." *The London government also demands an IRA surrender, as a precondition to dialogue with Sinn Féin. Yet, for over three years, the British government was involved in contact and dialogue with Sinn Féin without such preconditions*. The declared purpose of that contact was to explore the possibility of developing a real peace process. Now that they say they have such a possibility they cut the contact. Why? . . .

Sinn Féin has long accepted that northern Protestants have fears about their civil and religious liberties and we have consistently asserted that these liberties must be guaranteed and protected. Sinn Féin seeks a new Constitution for a new Ireland. This Constitution would include written guarantees and a Bill of Rights. What is required is an approach which creates political conditions in which, for the first time, the Irish people can reach a democratic accommodation, in which the consent and agreement of both nationalists and unionists can be achieved, in which a process of national reconciliation and healing can begin. Unionist participation in this is essential. . . .

It is with both governments that the main responsibility and authority rests. That is why we have consistently concentrated on trying to focus the governments on these issues. That is why we have refused to be sidetracked by the many distractions. One such distraction is whether Sinn Féin accepts what has been called the principle of consent.

There is much unnecessary confusion, as well as deliberate misrepresentation of the republican position on this point. We subscribe to, and I have no hesitation in reaffirming, the classical, democratic position of Irish nationalism. It was Britain that partitioned Ireland, turning the Irish unionist minority into an artificial majority in the Six-County area. Unionists are not—and do not claim to be—a nation with a right to national self-determination, as this is universally recognised in international law. Unionists are an Irish national minority, a religio/political minority, with minority rights not majority ones. Unionists can have no veto of British government policy or Irish government policy either for that matter.

The unionist position is in fact logically and politically an absurd one, for they in effect claim to possess a unilateral right to union with the British state, the majority of whose people do not want them, when there can only be unilateral rights of separation, never of union.

At the same time, while nationalists deny that unionists have any right of veto over British or Irish policy directed at seeking to dissolve the Union, most nationalists and republicans recognise as a matter of pragmatism that it is desirable in practice that the consent, or assent, of as many unionists as possible should be obtained to the steps that would be practically required to bring about the ending of partition and establishing a united Ireland.

These steps relate, of course, to the complex financial, constitutional and legal aspects of a final all-Ireland settlement, as well as other details and the time-scale involved. Republicans recognise that the national interest demands that the consent, or assent, of as many of our unionist fellow countrymen and fellow countrywomen as possible should be obtained to these steps. We believe indeed that the consent of the majority of present day unionists could in fact be won over time to these steps to reunification, provided that the two governments, and primarily the British government, made that the basis of their policy. That is why nationalists want Britain to "join the ranks of the persuaders," to base their policy on encouraging the coming together of

Protestants and Catholics, not underwriting our continued separation; as up to now.

My joint statements with John Hume have made very clear that the ultimate objective of the peace process in which we are involved seeks agreement among the divided peoples of Ireland, an agreement that must earn the allegiance, an agreement of all traditions and that both governments and all parties must be involved in this process.

The underlying assumption of these joint statements is that the only interest to be accommodated and the only problem to be resolved would be the division between the two main sections of the people who inhabit this island and that there would be no selfish British interests involved. But as the whole world knows, the view of republicans and nationalists, and it is a view which is historically correct, is that there are more serious elements in our problem and that these laments are selfish British interests.

British imperialism created the problem in the first place and has maintained it ever since. If we are now being told that this is no longer the case, that Britain has no longer any selfish interest in Ireland, and that the only problem today is the legacy of that past—the divisions among the people in Ireland—then it is obvious that this division can only be healed by agreement and it must be an agreement which earns the allegiance of all traditions, to quote again from my joint statements with John Hume.

But in these circumstances, is it not also reasonable for democrats to seek from the British government, given not only its responsibility for that legacy and its authority in the present situation that it should commit all its resources to heal that division and to promote agreement among our people?

Is it unreasonable to ask the British government what process, time-frame and frame-work it proposes for reaching such agreement?

Is it unreasonable to ask in advance what would be its reaction if any section of the people who inhabit our island refused to seek such agreement given the cost of disagreement not only to the Irish people but to the British people as well? And are these not reasonable requests, given that unionist politicians have never faced up to the central problem of reaching agreement with the rest of the people of this island and, in fact, have acted in collusion with the loyalist death squads to prevent such agreement? . . .

Republicans want peace. This generation of republicans seeks to see the gun taken out of Irish politics forever. If the British government commits itself to embracing and promoting the policy I have outlined here, then we republicans will commit all our energies and resources to reaching such an agreement. And, when such an agreement is reached, we will continue to use all our resources to promote the healing process that will be necessary to unite the Irish people in unity that will protect the democratic dignity, civil rights and heritage of all our people.

27. Gerry Adams Speech to Sinn Féin Ard Fheis (Annual Party Conference), 1997

Source: "Key Issues," CAIN, accessed 24 April 2019, https://cain.ulster.ac.uk/issues/politics/docs/sf/ga_1997.htm.

I want you to take a journey with me over the next short time, a journey of imagination, a journey of vision, a journey of time, a journey into the future. . . .

Imagine an Ireland in which the guns are silent. Permanently. An Ireland in which all of the people of this island are at peace with each other and with our neighbours in Britain.

Imagine an Ireland united by a process of healing and national reconciliation . . .

The search for a lasting peace has not succeeded so far. It was subverted but it cannot be crushed. It can only be postponed. The forces ranged against us are powerful but despite their power they have failed to defeat our struggle. They have failed to defeat our struggle because they fail to comprehend that the first step of liberation is in the human mind. Bobby Sands explained it well in one of the darkest moments of our struggle: "If they aren't able to destroy the desire for freedom, they won't break you." That is why centuries of British rule in Ireland has failed to subdue the struggle for independence and freedom. That is why they have failed to break us. . . .

Sinn Féin cannot be denied access to all party negotiations because of this threat from the Unionist leadership. If the Unionists do walk out they know the door will not be locked behind them. If they walk out they know they will have to walk back in again.

Peace is the issue here. When the British announce publicly that there can be no negotiations without yet another precondition, they merely echo the Unionist position on Sinn Féin's entrance to all party talks. They used the Unionists as an excuse. They encourage Unionist inertia. These exclusionist attitudes cannot create peace.

The Sinn Féin peace strategy, the Irish peace initiative, and the subsequent peace process are all part of our effort to change this. Sinn Féin know the lessons of the past. Irish republicanism is 200 years old next year and its principles are still relevant. The need to break the connection with England is as pertinent now as it was then. For Irish republicans the aim has never been the victory of one section of our people over another but a new union of Catholic, Protestant and Dissenter. It is not a pseudo peace—pax Britannica—but a real peace build [sic] on a solid democratic foundation and a future of justice and equality.

We have a vision of that future and the spirit and confidence to work in partnership with others to achieve this.

This means change.

Our task as republicans is to be agents of change; it is to build equality and partnership, and to empower change within our society. It is to change minds and attitudes and to rebuild relationships between the people of this island and with our nearest neighbour Britain. . . .

For us, and thus for everyone else there will be no going back to the bad old days of Unionist domination. There will be no going back to second class citizenship, there will be no return to Stormont rule.

Irish Republicans are prepared to do business, now, with the British government and with the unionists, without preconditions, without qualification, without delay. We are prepared to meet, to discuss and to reach agreement, to come to a democratic accommodation with unionism. But we are not prepared to pander to bigotry or the out-dated concepts of Orange supremacy and Unionist domination. We are not prepared to tolerate triumphalism and sectarianism. We will not be reconciled to the burning of churches and schools, to the denial of civil or religious liberties.

We make no apologies for this or for our commitment and our efforts to create a new political culture throughout this entire island. We stand for equality. We make no apologies for wanting an end to British rule and a new agreement between all the people of our island.

I want to speak directly to the Unionists. . . .

Republicans recognise that there will be no peace in Ireland if unionists are not a part of shaping that peace. Therefore our heartfelt wish is for a Unionism that is capable of shaping its future inside a negotiating process based upon equality. Our wish is to reach an accommodation with unionism.

This will not be easy. The road ahead will be difficult and dangerous and risky for all of us but working together I am convinced we can succeed. It is my conviction that we will have a peace settlement. If we are resilient, if we dig deep, we can overcome all obstacles. . . .

And of course dialogue is a two-way process. We actively listen but we also seek to inform. So Unionists need to see that Irish nationalists and republicans are forced to live in a British statelet which treats us as second class citizens. A statelet which for all of its existence has accorded the Orangemen the right to march through nationalist areas in triumphalistic coat-trailing and sectarian parades. There are also lots of reminders that the ethos which feeds this is not confined to the street or to working class loyalists. It permeates through the institutions of the six counties. These institutions remain faithful to Brookeborough's suffocating structure. Today the six counties are still run by Unionists for Unionists and policed by Unionists for Unionists.

But those days are numbered. . . .

Our objective is clear. It is to build a democracy which will be owned by every woman, man and child, on this island.

That means removing the causes of conflict from our country. British policy in Ireland has manifestly failed. One of the achievements of my dialogue with John Hume is our agreement that an internal settlement is not a solution. There is no going back to the failed policies and structures of the past, to the domination of a one-party unionist state supported by the British government.

How do we move forward? And brothers and sisters, let there be no doubt about that we must move forward. How do we do it? How do we fulfil the potential, the ideals and dreams, so that our children and our children's children can enjoy peace and justice?

Sinn Féin is absolutely committed to democratic and peaceful methods of resolving problems and part of our responsibility is to make alliances with others, to help chart the journey forward, to illuminate the way and to work with the people of Ireland to establish beacons or guide-lines, based on international experiences, to help us all to traverse this period of transition. We are on a journey from the past into a new future.

Irish freedom, democracy and peace are in the interests of all the people on the island. Partition effects [sic] all of us. Sinn Féin seeks national self-determination, and the unity and independence of Ireland as a sovereign state.

In our view this issue of sovereignty, the claim of the British government to sovereignty in Ireland, is the key matter which must be addressed in any negotiation.

There are some who say the British government is neutral. Whatever about its strategic or economic interest, John Major has made it clear that he is a defender of the Union. This policy and the Unionist veto are at the core of the conflict.

The aim of democratic opinion must be to seek a change in British policy towards Ireland and an end to the Unionist veto. Negotiations are an area of struggle for Irish republicans.

There are many issues which fuel the conflict which must be tackled but which do not require negotiation. For example, parity of esteem and equality of treatment will have to be dealt with; the imbalance in the employment ratio; equality in economic development; greater and more equally shared prosperity; the Irish language and culture need equality of treatment; there is a long overdue need to bring about the empowerment and inclusion of deprived and marginalised communities. These should be pursued inside and outside negotiations.

The whole issue of demilitarisation needs to be resolved. This includes the release of all political prisoners. The treatment of convicted killers from the British Army in comparison, for example, with the treatment of untried, remand prisoner, Roisin McAliskey, is proof of British double standards. Disarmament, policing, the administration of justice and an end to repressive legislation also needs to be tackled. . . .

Sinn Féin seeks change. We are not afraid of change. We have embraced change. It is the lifeblood of political struggle and the basis for a lasting peace agreement. Our task must be to make change irreversible. Some time ago, in a spirit of generosity and in an effort to create a space in which progress could be made I made it clear, in the context of proper all-party talks and in a situation in which all the other parties sign up to the Mitchell Report, that Sinn Féin will do so also.

We ask no more than is accorded to any other party, open and honest dialogue, everyone at the table, everything on the table and no Unionist veto. For us there is no room for failure. . . .

Sinn Féin is an essential key component in any lasting peace settlement. We stand ready to play our part.

SECTION G. CROSS-COMMUNITY POLITICAL DOCUMENT OF THE 1990S

28. Alliance Party of Northern Ireland, "Multiparty Talks: Principles and Realities of a Settlement," 13 October 1997

Source: "Principles of Agreement," Alliance Party of Northern Ireland, 13 October 1997, https://www.allianceparty.org/peace_process_papers.

In our initial presentation of the Alliance Analysis of the Problem and its origins we outlined some fundamental principles which inform our approach. These principles express very concisely what are, for us, the minimum necessary requirements for a solution to our difficulties. . . .

1. Community Government

Our first principle expressed the conviction that, despite the obvious divisions, the people of Northern Ireland form a community. Like any other such community, these people have the right to determine their own future, and participate directly in their own governance. For this reason it is very strongly our view that a provincial or regional government is necessary, to provide a common focus of identity, and an opportunity to share in self-government. . . .

On the more negative side, uncertainty and ambiguity provoke anxiety and give encouragement to those who thrive on fear. Any settlement must therefore remove negative uncertainties. The acknowledgement by the two governments of the principle of consent is a clear statement of the right of the Northern Ireland community to self-determination, and a tacit acknowledgement that the present wish of that community as a whole is to remain within the United Kingdom. . . . Openness and transparency, are the enemies of the fears fed by ignorance and confusion. These must also be key principles in the establishing of any settlement, and indeed of this Talk Process.

Given that there are, as in every community, different identities, and particularly since at least some of these distinctions have, in Northern Ireland, been pushed to the point of division, it is necessary to create common institutions and instruments of government in which all can participate and with which all can identify. We take the view that an elected assembly, with legislative as well as executive functions in an extensive range of areas (giving significant socio-economic autonomy), including relationships with the Republic of Ireland is the minimum necessary to provide this unifying factor. It would be Profoundly [*sic*] counter-productive if in the construction of such structures the very divisions which they were established to heal were institutionalised by the forms of protection they used. For this reason setting out two separate sets of mirroring rights, with parity of esteem between only two traditions, and insisting on always dividing people into Protestant and Catholic, and unionist and nationalist (and assuming also that these divisions are contiguous), would not be a healing of the divisions but an institutionalising of them. Instead we should recognise one set of rights that applies to everyone, one community with a number of rich, overlapping strands of culture and tradition, and recognition of an inclusive pluralism of religious and political thought and adherence which does not marginalise the partners and children of mixed marriages, the values of integrated education, and interdenominational religious activities, and political liberals who do not espouse nationalism or one kind or another. Everyone must be able to be confident of equality of treatment.

2. Everyone Involved and Protected

This naturally leads to our second fundamental Alliance principle. This presented our primary objective to be the protection and the valuing of minorities. There are a number of ways in which this can be achieved.

Firstly, of course, all elected representatives can press the case for their people on the floor of an assembly, or in committees. All elections to a regional assembly, and to the membership and chairmanship of any committees of such an assembly must be on a proportionate basis so that all are treated equally fairly.

The prospect of being involved in government must be open to any democratic politician from any part of the community. In many societies including, one could argue, the rest of the United Kingdom and the Republic of Ireland, the expedient of the "simple majority" creates the prospect of changing the government. This is the principle upon which the Westminster system was constructed, right down to the arrangement of seating in the House of Commons, (though not of course the House of Lords where there is a significant cross-bench component). Much of this system was adopted by the Republic of Ireland. In Northern Ireland during the period 1922–1972, the Westminster-based system created not one single change in the political profile of government. Elections were in that sense so meaningless that on occasions they were not even contested in some seats. In order to ensure that elections are meaningful such arrangements must be modified. Modifications such as weighted majorities have been mentioned in this regard, and we believe that, applied in the formation of the government and in the passage of legislation, could fulfil the necessary requirements.

All of these proposals deal with the positive aspect of involvement of minorities (and majorities), but there is also a need for protections. The best machinery would be the establishment, entrenchment and enforcement of a Bill of Rights, accountable through our own courts. Further political protection of groups could be achieved by the creation of a Political Right of Appeal, whereby a certain proportion of members of the assembly could appeal to a separate authority for arbitration.

3. Rule of Law

The third of the fundamental principles set out in the Alliance founding document in 1970 begins as follows: "We firmly believe that without universal respect for the law of the land and the authorities appointed to enforce it, there can be no measurable progress. We believe that this is not only a self-evident principle, but also one which commands widespread support in all sections of the community. The major problem remains, how to achieve such respect.

Some of the requirements mentioned above will help, but it is also necessary to deal directly with the control and execution of justice and security policy. . . .

There is no future for the Northern Ireland community, no security for any family or individual, and no prospect of economic improvement without respect for the Rule of Law.

4. The Totality of Relations

In these talks we have to consider the requirements of relations with the rest of the United Kingdom (Strand One), the Republic of Ireland (largely Strand Two), between the United Kingdom and the Republic of Ireland (Strand Three), and the rest of the European Community (Strands One, Two, and Three). . . . What are some of the practical requirements which these principles might suggest?

In relation with the rest of the United Kingdom, we would accept that there could usefully be some clarification of the lines of communications, the channels of influence, and the levels of accountability, between a new provincial/regional government and the sovereign government, and between the Westminster MPs elected from Northern Ireland, and the elected representatives of an assembly. The emergence of differing regional institutions in Scotland and Wales, and probably in London and elsewhere, will ensure that this element of our discussions may be usefully informed by the experience of others.

Relations with the Government of the Republic of Ireland will require changes to Articles 2 & 3 of the constitution of the Republic, but given that prospect we would see it as important that a direct, standing, North/South, government to government relationship, be established, and exemplified by joint commissions on areas of shared practical interest, e.g. agriculture, energy, tourism etc. . . .

The growth and development of the European Union, convince us that it is vital that we are able grasp the opportunities offered by this broader framework. To see ourselves as all living within a larger border, rather than living on either sides of various geographical and political dividing lines, opens up the prospect of an increasing sense of shared experience. The economic necessity of representing our people will also help to bind us together as a Northern Ireland community. . . .

5. Permanence and Stability

After so many years, and indeed generations of violence and instability our people long for a settled peace. The permanence and stability of any agreed outcome will be considerably enhanced by its direct endorsement by the people, but if it is to survive the heady endorsement of a referendum, it must also be workable in practice, carry out the business of political life in an efficient and effective manner, and not be dependent on any particular electoral outcome or inter-party deal.

Clearly the people of Northern Ireland have a primary interest in these issues, but the people of the Republic of Ireland also have a very real interest, and in any case they must express their view positively in a referendum, if there is to be any change, as we maintain there must be, in Articles 2 & 3 of the Republic's constitution. The construction of such a test of public opinion is not a simple matter and will require a good deal of thought and discussion.

IMAGES OF THE TROUBLES: WHERE TO FIND FILMS, MURALS, AND PHOTOGRAPHS

A major source of primary documents, secondary articles, images, and other materials related to the conflict and peace process in Northern Ireland can be found at the website hosted by Ulster University: CAIN Archive, Conflict and Politics in Northern Ireland: https://cain.ulster.ac.uk/index.html. Posters and murals painted on the sides of buildings in Northern Ireland were important statements in claiming urban territory, expressing communal values, and urging populations to defense or revenge. Most of the murals painted during the 1968–98 period have since been painted over with new images. But while some of the new art helps to carry the call for peace and reconciliation, much of it still carries Unionist or National messages. Your GM may provide you with access to photographs of murals taken in 2020 by John Burney. Additional images can be found in CAIN collections: for photographs, see https://cain.ulster.ac.uk/photographs/index.html; for mural images, see https://cain.ulster.ac.uk/mural. Students can also consult *Murals of Derry* (Derry: Guildhall Press, rev. ed. 2016). The YouTube site "Northern Ireland Conflict Videos" uploads contemporary news clips and documentaries from both communities on its website: https://www.youtube.com/@NorthernIrelandConflictVideos/about.

Acknowledgments

The authors would like to thank those faculty and students who participated in the play tests of "Ending the Troubles" as it has developed starting at Loras College in 2019; at the Institute of Art Design and Technology in Dun Laoghaire, Dublin, Ireland, in March 2020; the online Reacting to the Past Game Development Conference in July 2021; the Midwest Regional American Conference for Irish Studies in October 2021at Northern Illinois University; and the Reacting to the Past Summer Institute at Barnard College in June 2023. We would also like to thank those faculty and Reacting veterans who provided us with more detailed feedback, including Christopher Budzisz, David Cochran, John Eby, Kasee Laster, Kelly McFall, Erik Mustad, Nick Proctor, Mary Robinson, Mary Jane Treacy, and John Waldmeir, as well as our mapmaker Catherine Koetz and Andrew Winters at UNC Press. A special appreciation to our spouses, LouAnn Dunklau Burney and Mary Ellen McKinstra-Auge, for supporting and indulging our retirement project.

Notes

INTRODUCTION

1. Tony Parker, *May the Lord in His Mercy Be Kind to Belfast* (London: HarperCollins, 1993), 294.

HISTORICAL BACKGROUND

1. Thomas Cahill, *How the Irish Saved Civilization* (New York: Anchor, 2010).
2. The bull is found in Charles Carlton, *Bigotry and Blood: Documents on the Ulster Troubles* (Chicago: Nelson-Hall, 1977), 4-5.
3. Thomas E. Hachey, Joseph M. Hernon Jr., and Lawrence J. McCaffrey, *The Irish Experience: A Concise History*, rev. ed. (London: M. E. Sharpe, 1996), 15.
4. For an analysis of the impact of the Penal Laws, see Ultán Gillen, "Ascendancy Ireland," in *The Princeton History of Modern Ireland*, ed. Richard Bourke and Ian McBride, 55-59 (Princeton, NJ: Princeton University Press, 2016).
5. Wolfe Tone, *Argument on Behalf of the Catholics of Ireland*, CELT: The Corpus of Electronic Texts, accessed 1 July 2019, https://celt.ucc.ie//published/E790002/index.html.
6. Ciara Boylan, "Famine," in Bourke and McBride, *Princeton History of Modern Ireland*, 413.
7. See Hachey, Hernon, and McCaffrey, *The Irish Experience*, 128; and Matthew Kelly, "Nationalisms," in Bourke and McBride, *Princeton History of Modern Ireland*, 447-69.
8. Charles Townshend, *Ireland in the 20th Century* (London: Arnold, 1998), 19.
9. Townshend, *Ireland in the 20th Century*, 43-44.
10. Hachey, Hernon, and McCaffrey, *Irish Experience*, 138-44.
11. Townshend, *Ireland in the 20th Century*, 57-61.
12. Marc Mulholland, *Northern Ireland: A Very Short Introduction* (Oxford: Oxford University Press, 2002), 19.
13. Quoted in Ulrich O'Connor, *Michael Collins and the Troubles: The Struggle for Irish Freedom, 1912-1922* (New York: Norton, 1996), 50.
14. Quoted in O'Connor, 74-74. On the motivations of the uprising, see also Ferghal McGarry, *The Rising, Ireland: Easter 1916* (Oxford: Oxford University Press, 2010), 95-102; and Clair Wills, *Dublin 1916: The Siege of the GPO* (Cambridge, MA: Harvard University Press, 2009), 52-57.
15. Quoted in Townshend, *Ireland in the 20th Century*, 84. See also McGarry, *Rising*, 279-86.
16. Quoted in Feargal Cochrane, *Northern Ireland: The Reluctant Peace* (New Haven, CT: Yale University Press, 2013), 35.
17. Marie-Therese Fay, Mike Morrissey, and Marie Smythe, *Northern Ireland's Troubles: The Human Cost* (London: Pluto, 1999), 78.
18. Fay, Morrissey, and Smythe, *Northern Ireland's Troubles*, 169.
19. Peter Taylor, *Loyalists: War and Peace in Northern Ireland* (New York: TV Books, 1999), 17.
20. Kevin Toolis, *Rebel Hearts: Journeys within the IRA's Soul* (London: St. Martin's Griffin, 1995), 53.
21. David McKittrick and David McVea, *Making Sense of the Troubles: The Story of the Conflict in Northern Ireland* (Chicago: New Amsterdam, 2002), 13.
22. "Ian Paisley in Quotes," BBC, accessed 17 May 2023, www.bbc.com/news/uk-northernireland.
23. McKittrick and McVea, *Making Sense of the Troubles*, 59.
24. McKittrick and McVea, *Making Sense of the Troubles*, 68.
25. McKittrick and McVea, *Making Sense of the Troubles*, 123.
26. McKittrick and McVea, *Making Sense of the Troubles*, 141.
27. Quoted in Paul Dixon and Eamonn O'Kane, *Northern Ireland since 1969* (London: Routledge, 2011), 51-52.
28. Paul Bew and Gordon Gillespie, *Northern Ireland: A Chronology of the Troubles 1968-1999* (Lanham, MD: Scarecrow, 1999), 185.
29. Bew and Gillespie, *Northern Ireland*, 190.
30. Bew and Gillespie, *Northern Ireland*, 191.
31. McKittrick and McVea, *Making Sense of the Troubles*, 123-24.
32. Bew and Gillespie, *Northern Ireland*, 242.
33. "Address by Prime Minister Tony Blair at the Royal Agricultural Society Belfast, 16 May 1997," CAIN, accessed 27 July 2019, https://cain.ulster.ac.uk/events/peace/docs/tb16597.htm.

THE GAME

1. John McGarry and Brendan O'Leary, *Explaining Northern Ireland* (Oxford, UK: Blackwell, 1995), 184–89, 270.

2. Anthony D. Smith, *Nationalism*, 2nd ed. (Cambridge, UK: Polity, 2010), 9.

3. Martin Melaugh, "An Outline of the Main 'Solutions' to the Conflict," CAIN, accessed 11 April 2023, https://cain.ulster.ac.uk/issues/politics/polsol.htm.

Selected Bibliography

Adams, Gerry. *Cage Eleven: Writings from Prison*. Boulder, CO: Roberts Rinehart, 1990.

Anderson, Benedict. *Imagined Communities: Reflections on the Origins and Spread of Nationalism*. 2nd ed. London: Verso, 1991.

Armstrong, Charles, David Herbert, and Jan Erik Mustad, eds. *The Legacy of the Good Friday Agreement: Northern Irish Politics, Culture, and Art after 1998*. Cham, Switzerland: Palgrave Macmillan, 2019.

Aughey, Arthur, and Cathy Gormley-Heenan, eds. *The Anglo-Irish Agreement: Rethinking Its Legacy*. Manchester, UK: Manchester University Press, 2011.

Bartlett, Thomas. *Ireland: A History*. Cambridge: Cambridge University Press, 2010.

Beresford, David. *Ten Men Dead: The Story of the 1981 Irish Hunger Strike*. New York: Atlantic Monthly Press, 1987.

Bew, Paul, and Gordon Gillespie. *Northern Ireland: A Chronology of the Troubles, 1968-1999*. Lanham, MD: Scarecrow, 1999.

Bourke, Richard, and Ian McBride, eds. *The Princeton History of Modern Ireland*. Princeton, NJ: Princeton University Press, 2016.

Boyle, Ken, and Tom Hadden. *Northern Ireland: The Choice*. London: Penguin, 1994.

Carlton, Charles. *Bigotry and Blood: Documents on the Ulster Troubles*. Chicago: Nelson-Hall, 1977.

Cash, John D. *Identity, Ideology, and Conflict: The Structuration of Politics in Northern Ireland*. Cambridge: Cambridge University Press, 1996.

Cochrane, Feargal. *Northern Ireland: The Fragile Pace*. New ed. New Haven, CT: Yale University Press, 2021.

———. *Northern Ireland: The Reluctant Peace*. New Haven, CT: Yale University Press, 2013.

Conroy, John. *Belfast Diary: War as a Way of Life*. Boston: Beacon, 1995.

De Barra, Caoimhin. *The Coming of the Celts, A.D. 1860*. Notre Dame: University of Notre Dame Press, 2018.

Dillon, Martin. *God and the Gun: The Church and Irish Terrorism*. New York: Routledge, 1997.

Dixon, Paul, and Eamonn O'Kane. *Northern Ireland since 1969*. London: Routledge, 2011.

English, Richard. *Armed Struggle: The History of the IRA*. Oxford: Oxford University Press, 2003.

Fay, Marie-Therese, Mike Morrissey, and Marie Smythe. *Northern Ireland's Troubles: The Human Costs*. London: Pluto, 1999.

Fearon, Kate. *Woman's Work: The Story of the Northern Ireland Women's Coalition*. Belfast: Blackstaff, 1999.

Foster, R. F. *Modern Ireland, 1600-1972*. London: Penguin, 1988.

Hachey, Thomas E., Joseph M. Hernon Jr., and Lawrence J. McCaffrey. *The Irish Experience: A Concise History*. Rev. ed. London: M. E. Sharpe, 1996.

Hume, John. *A New Ireland: Politics, Peace, and Reconciliation*. Boulder, CO: Roberts Rinehart, 1996.

Hutchinson, John. *The Dynamics of Cultural Nationalism: The Gaelic Revival and the Creation of the Irish Nation-State*. London: Allen & Unwin, 1987.

"IRA: Behind the Mask." PBS and WBGH *Frontline*, 1998. https://www.youtube.com/watch?v=zAal17smUAw.

Jackson, Alvin. *Ireland, 1798-1998. War, Peace, and Beyond*. 2nd ed. London: Wiley-Blackwell, 2010.

Keefe, Patrick Radden. *Say Nothing: A True Story of Murder and Memory in Northern Ireland*. New York: Doubleday, 2019.

Lijphart, Arend. *Democracy in Plural Societies*. New Haven, CT: Yale University Press, 1977.

McEvoy, Joanne. *The Politics of Northern Ireland*. Edinburgh: Edinburgh University Press, 2008.

McGarry, John, ed. *Northern Ireland and the Divided World*. New York: Oxford University Press, 2001.

McGarry, John, and Brendan O'Leary. *Explaining Northern Ireland*. Oxford: Blackwell, 1995.

McKittrick, David, and David McVea. *Making Sense of the Troubles: A History of the Northern Ireland Conflict*. London: Viking, 2012.

Mulholland, Marc. *Northern Ireland: A Very Short Introduction*. Oxford: Oxford University Press, 2002.

O'Connor, Ulrich. *Michael Collins and the Troubles: The Struggle for Irish Freedom, 1912-1922*. New York: Norton, 1996.

O'Neill, Eimhar. *Wave Goodbye to the Dinosaurs*. Harrow, UK: Taskovski Films, 2018. https://www.taskovskifilms.com/film/wave-goodbye-to-dinosaurs.

O'Toole, Fintan. *We Don't Know Ourselves: A Personal History of Ireland*. New York: Norton, 2021.

Parker, Tony. *May the Lord in His Mercy Be Kind to Belfast*. London: HarperCollins, 1993.

Paseta, Senia. *Modern Ireland: A Very Short Introduction*. Oxford: Oxford University Press, 2003.

Power, Maria. *Catholic Social Teaching and Theologies of Peace in Northern Ireland: Cardinal Cahal Daly and the Pursuit of a Peaceable Kingdom*. London: Routledge, 2021.

Sands, Bobby. *Writings from Prison*. 1983. Boulder, CO: Roberts Rinehart, 1997.

Shannon, Elizabeth. *I Am of Ireland: Women of the North Speak Out*. Rev. ed. Amherst: University of Massachusetts Press, 1997.

Smith, Anthony D. *Nationalism*. 2nd ed. Cambridge, UK: Polity, 2010.

Smithey, Lee A. *Unionists, Loyalists, & Conflict Transformation in Northern Ireland*. Oxford: Oxford University Press, 2011.

Taylor, Peter. *Behind the Mask: The IRA and Sinn Féin*. New York: TV Books, 1997.

———. "Loyalists." Northern Ireland Conflict Videos, episode 2, YouTube, accessed 28 March 2024, https://www.youtube.com/watch?v=000biYnVBE8.

———. *Loyalists: War and Peace in Northern Ireland*. New York: TV Books, 1999.

Toolis, Kevin. *Rebel Hearts: Journeys within the IRA's Soul*. New York: St. Martin's Griffin, 1995.

Townshend, Charles. *Ireland in the Twentieth Century*. London: Arnold, 1998.

Wills, Clair. *Dublin 1916: The Siege of the GPO*. Cambridge, MA: Harvard University Press, 2009.

www.ingramcontent.com/pod-product-compliance
Lightning Source LLC
Chambersburg PA
CBHW080636230426
43663CB00016B/2896